D0705659

MOUNT ATHOS

Publishers: George A. Christopoulos, John C. Bastias
Translation: Louise Turner
Managing Editor: Efi Karpodini
Art Director: Nicos Andricakis
Special Photography: M. Skiadaresis and N. Kontos, A. Spyropoulos, Th. Provatakis

Reproduction, printing and binding: Ekdotike Ellados S.A., 8, Philadelphias St.

MOUNT ATHOS

An illustrated guide to the monasteries and their history

SOTIRIS KADAS
Archaeologist

EKDOTIKE ATHENON S.A.
Athens 1993

97/1549

CONTENTS

GULF OF IERISSOS

Ierissos

N.Roda

Amoliani

Ouranoupolis

Chromitsa

C

N. Theba

SINGITIC GULF

STRYMONIC GULF

Koronia L.

Volvi L.

Rendina

SALONIKA

C H A L K I D I K I

Stageira

Stratonike

THERMAIC GULF

Vassilika

Galatista

Mt Cholomon

Ierissos

N. Roda

HOLY MOUNT

Polygyros

Arnea

Ouranoupolis

N. Thebais

Amoliani

SINGITIC GULF

N. Kallikratia

Olynthos

Ag. Nikolaos

Daphn

N. Moudania

N. Potidea

GULF OF KASSANDRA

SITHONIA

N. Marmaras

Sarte

Kassandria

KASSANDRA
(PALLINI)

Toroni

Possidi

Paliouri

THE PENINSULA OF MOUNT ATHOS

Monasteries

Sketae

Dependencies

GRAPHOU

VATOPEDI

ST DEMETRIOS

AMONITOU

BOGORODITSA

PANTOKRATOROS

DOCHIARIOU

PROPHET ELIJAH

ST ANDREW

STAVRONIKITA

XENOPHONTOS

KARYES

ST PANTELEIMON

ANNUNCIATION

KOUTLOUMOUSIOU

IVIRON

SAINT PANTELEIMON

XEROPOTAMOU

PRODROMOU

Daphne

KARAKALOU

PHILOTHEOU

SIMONOPETRA

ST DEMETRIOS

GREGORIOU

DIONYSIOU

GRANDE LAVRA

SAINT-PAUL

Mt Athos

NEW SKETE

Kerasia

Eremos

ST ANNE

St Basil

PRODROMOU

Katounakia

KAVSOKALYVIA

Little St Anne

Karoulia

os

FROM LEGEND TO HISTORY

Athos is the easternmost of the three promontories of Chalkidiki – a Greek peninsula that stretches into the Aegean Sea between the Thermaic and Strimonic gulfs. Some 60 kilometres in length, Athos varies in width from 8-12 kilometres covering in all an area of approximately 360 square kilometres. The landward end of the promontory is low and flat, with small plains and hillocks; but as it extends seawards, clusters of peaks swell higher and higher to end finally in the bare slopes of Mount Athos, whose pyramidal summit rises sheer from the sea to more than 2000 metres.

The ancients called the whole peninsula *Akte*. The name Athos, a prehellenic word, was that of a Thracian giant who, according to one view, hurled that whole stony mass at Poseidon in a clash between gods and giants. In another version of the Gigantomachy, we are told that Poseidon was victorious, burying the rebellious giant Athos under the great rock. According to another legend, first recorded by Strabo and repeated by Plutarch, Deinokrates, architect to Alexander the Great, wanted to transform the whole of Mount Athos into an immense figure of the Macedonian king. The sculptured effigy was to hold in one hand a city swarming with people, while from the other a copious stream of water would gush towards the sea as a continuous libation to the gods. Alexander declined the offer and ordered that the mountain should be left as it was, perhaps because he did not wish to appear to his descendants as arrogant as the Persian King Xerxes. In 481 B.C. Xerxes cut a canal through the narrow neck of land at the beginning of the peninsula, between the Ierissos and the Singitic gulfs, so that his fleet should avoid the stormy waters round Cape Akrothoos where earlier the ships of the Persian general Mardonius had sunk. Some historians doubt that the cutting was ever completed, while others dispute that it was ever undertaken. The latter claim that Xerxes transported his fleet overland on wooden rollers.

During the centuries that follow, little – very little, indeed – is known of the history of Athos. Sources refer to several small towns or 'small settlements' there, such as Sani, Thissos, Kleonae, Dion, Olophixos, Akrothooi, and Apollonia, whose exact locations have not been determined. But we know for certain that, although they prospered for a while, they must have been already in ruins by the time the first hermits came to the Mountain.

1. Katounakia, a monastic settlement at Eremos, with isolated kalyves and hermitages.

MONASTICISM ON MOUNT ATHOS

Monasticism is the individual's renunciation of the world and his retreat into a solitary life to achieve the salvation of his soul through contemplation and closer communion with God. Christian monasticism originated at the beginning of the fourth century, as a reaction to the prevailing social corruption. The way was already paved by the gospel teaching, the tendency towards Judaic ascetism and the spirit of contemporary Greek philosophy. Above all, however, monasticism grew apace because of the persecution of Christians by the state during the preceding three centuries. The keystones of monastic life are the virtues of chastity, poverty and obedience. These ideals are achieved by continual bodily and spiritual exercises, and through an absolute and unquestioning devotion to God.

Monastic communities first appeared and flourished in Egypt, Syria and Asia Minor. Others were founded later in Palestine and Constantinople. Many have since disappeared. The few still in existence are either in ruins or are inhabited by a mere handful of monks existing in what remains of their past magnificence. Though founded later than those mentioned above, the sole monastic centre which can claim a continuous and unbroken history is Mount Athos. Its monasteries remain today, what they have always been, the cradle of Orthodoxy and the bastion of Eastern Christianity.

Legend reveals to us how the Mother of God became celestial patron and protectress of Mount Athos. According to one tradition, the Virgin Mary, accompanied by St John the Evangelist, was on her way to visit Lazaros in Cyprus, when a sudden storm arose and her ship was carried by a violent wind to Athos. They are said to have come ashore close to the present monastery of Iveron. There the Holy Virgin rested for a while, and, overwhelmed by the beauty of the place, she asked her Son to give her the Mountain, despite the fact that its inhabitants were pagans. In response, a voice was heard saying: 'let this place be your inheritance and your garden, a paradise and a haven of salvation for those seeking to be saved'. Thus the Holy Mountain was consecrated as the inheritance and garden of the Mother of God.

Athos was an area eminently suited to those wishing to practise the rigours of an ascetic life, and from the earliest years of the Byzantine period it attracted men from all parts of the Empire. By the Middle Byzantine period the whole peninsula was commonly known as the Holy Mountain, a name officially adopted and confirmed in a special chrysobull of the Emperor Constantine IX Monomachos (1046). Other similar monastic centres, where there were groups of monasteries, such as Sinai and Olympos in Bithynia, were referred to by this same term.

The exact date of the first monastic settlement on Athos cannot be determined. Neither can we be very specific about the development and dissemination of monastic life. The information available today, especially for the period before the ninth century, is not only scanty and sporadic, but is, for the most part, based on traditions and legends. The Athonite monks themselves claim Constantine the Great as the founder of certain monasteries, later destroyed by Julian the Apostate, only to be built again by Theodosius the Great and Pulcheria. With a degree of certainty we can assert that contemplatives had already begun to frequent the Mountain by the seventh century.

Apart from the reasons previously mentioned, the development of monasticism on Athos was strongly influenced by three historical factors: the break-up of the earliest village communities; the Arab conquests; and anti-monastic feeling. The decline of the small towns in the vicinity of Mount Athos and the deser-

2. *The monasteries of Mount Athos in an engraving of 1889. (Athens, National Gallery).*

tion of the peninsula turned it into an attractive place for those inclined to contemplation and religious devotion. The advances and conquests of the Arabs in
the eastern countries, and the consequent ruin of the big monastic centres
there, forced the dispersal of their many monks. These men hastened to seek
new lands on which to re-establish their monasteries and continue their ascetic
way of life. Lastly, Athos became an ark of refuge from the hostility emanating
from the Byzantine emperors and the inhabitants of Constantinople towards
monks and monasticism in general, especially during the iconoclastic period.

The Holy Mountain first appears as a monastic centre in the historical sources
of the ninth century. It is recorded that monks from Athos participated in the
Council of 843 convened by the Empress Theodora to discuss the restoration
of the holy icons. At about the same time we come to know the names of two
men who mere influential in the history of Athos, Peter the Athonite and Euthymios of Salonica. These two men, nearly contemporaries, represented different
ascetic trends; Peter the eremetical and Euthymios the semi-eremetical. The
reputations of these two men attracted recruits to the Mountain, and Athos began to emerge as a notable monastic centre, modelled on the communities of
the East and those which existed in, or near, Constantinople. In 885 the chrysobull of the Emperor Basil I officially recognised Athos as a territory belonging ex-
clusively to monks and hermits. It laid down that only men of religion should live
there, and that henceforward all shepherds and laymen who until that time had
roamed freely there, should be forbidden the 'Garden of the Virgin'.

Although it is not possible to reach any certain conclusions about the ante-
cedents of organised monastic life on Athos, we may supose that Athonite

monasticism followed the same pattern of development as other monastic centres. That is to say, it developed within a relatively short space of time from the eremetical to the semi-eremetical stage, and from there to the coenobitic form. Thus the hermits first established themselves at the landward end of the peninsula where the terrain is gentle. Later, fleeing from the various raiders, especially the Saracen pirates, the solitaries abandoned this area: some sought the greater security of the peaks, others the protection of almost inaccessible slopes. Later still, hermits grouped into loosely organised communities, the *lavras*, modelled after those of Palestine. The names of two such communities are known to us; Clementos, near the present day monastery of Iveron, and the more important 'Assembly of the Elders' (the *Kathedra)* on the heights of Zygos, of which we shall speak in more detail later. The third stage, the coenobitic, took root in the ninth century with the founding of a monastery near Ierissos by John, abbot of Kolobos. The coenobitic life was firmly established about a century later with the building of the Great Lavra by Athanasios.

The monks of the 'Assembly of the Elders', gathered together for communal worship in a central church (the *katholikon).* The leaders from each of its constituent cells formed an assembly – *synaxis* – which met whenever necessary, and at least three times a year at the feasts of Christmas, Easter and the Dormition of the Virgin. At these councils, over which the *Protos* presided, matters of common interest mere debated. In a chrysobull of Romanos I Lekapenos (934), the *kathedra* is described as 'ancient', which shows that it had been in existence sometime before, and certainly since the ninth century. During the tenth century, as we shall see below, new monasteries were founded. These attracted many monks, with the result that the numbers of the *kathedra* diminished, declining to the point where the community all but disintegrated. This new turn of events forced the *Protos* to transfer his seat closer to the centre of the peninsula, to the area called Mesi, later named Karyes, where it has remained ever since.

Although Kolobos had intoduced the coenobitic life, it was decisively established by Athanasios the Athonite. Friend and confessor of the Emperor Nicephoros Phocas, Athanasios founded about 963 the famous monastery of the Great Lavra with monies provided by the emperor himself. Thus the wattle huts were replaced by great stone edifices and the eremetical life by an organised, communal one. This innovation, however, provoked a storm of protest from many Athonites, incuding those dwelling in loosely organised *lavras (Lavriotes).* Their leader was the powerful and uncompromising personality, the monk Paul Xeropotaminos. A Byzantine of noble birth, Paul conceived the ascetic life in its most austere form: escape to the wilderness, total withdrawal from secular life, absolute solitude. He eschewed involvement in temporal affairs, and shunned participation in great deeds. Athanasios, on the contrary, though no less pious and virtuous, was a man of broader outlook, with wide-ranging administrative talents. Although not opposed to the solitary life, he considered communal activities and the interdependence of monks no less important.

It was inevitable that these two men, representing contrary approaches to the monastic life, should clash. Paul Xeropotaminos, accompanied by other monks, departed for Constantinople in order to protest against Athanasios to the Emperor John Tzimisces. He claimed that Athanasios had brought luxury to the Mountain, broken its ancient customs and norms and given a worldly aspect to the holy place. The emperor despatched a monk, Euthymios Studitis, to investigate these allegations. But Euthymios, being a friend of Athanasios, naturally found in his favour, to the extent of recognising the forms and rights

3. The port of Daphne where pilgrims coming from Ouranopolis land.

of the big monasteries. These decisions confirmed the rules and disciplines of Athanasios, and were embodied in the first *Typikon* (Charter) (971/2), which still governs life on Athos today.

With this wider concept of monasticism, Athanasios attracted the following of many hermits who lived in isolation in separate dwellings. Amongst them were Georgians, Armenians and Latins. Indeed, at the instigation of St Athanasios, the latter founded the monastery of the Virgin of the Amalfians, near Morphonou, a small bay north of Great Lavra. This monastery owes its name to the inhabitants of the Amalfi quarter of Constantinople, who came from southern Italy and who supported the monastery financially. It was eventually deserted as a result of the hostile attitude of the Orthodox towards the Latins, and only its magnificent tower remains.

In addition to Great Lavra, two other large monasteries were established in the tenth century, Vatopedi and Iveron. Several smaller ones were founded, including Docheiariou, Philotheou and Xenophontos, and others which today are known only as names.

In the eleventh century, when the coenobitic life on the Mountain had been firmly established, more monasteries were founded, and their number reached 180. In reality, however, most of these foundations more closely resembled large *kellia*, and not monasteries in their present form. But from the end of the century, and especially during the reign of the Emperor Alexios Comnenos I, the vigour of Athonite monasticism was undermined by frequent pirate raids in which many monasteries were pillaged and others totally destroyed. During this period the Mountain suffered incursions, fortunately only for a short time, by Vlach shepherds who upset its peaceful monastic life. This fact is mentioned in a chrysobull of Alexios I in which, among other matters, every female human or animal, was forbidden entry to the Mountain.

During the twelfth century fewer monastic houses were founded, but numerous existing *kellia* expanded into monasteries. Increasing numbers of monks of other nationalities – Iberians (Georgians), Latins, Serbs and Russians – all having in common the link of Orthodox Christianity, came to share the Mountain in worship.

During the thirteenth century, the period of the Latin Occupation (1204-61), the Mountain suffered in common with the rest of the Byzantine Empire from the Frankish raids. These came to an end only when the Paleologue dynasty re-established Constantinople as capital of the Empire. During the years following the Latin conquest, Mount Athos was replaced under the jurisdiction of the Latin Kingdom of Salonica, and the monks were subjected to much pressure to accept the Union of the two churches, East and West. These pressures unfortunately continued long after 1261, and were exerted by Michael VIII and the Patriarch John Vekkos, both Unionists. In their effort to 'latinise' the monks, they despoiled the monasteries, destroyed the churches and tortured a number of monks. They went so far as to execute Athonite fathers in the Protaton, at the monasteries of Vatopedi, Zographou, and elsewhere.

After the death of the Emperor Michael, however, life on the Mountain resumed its normal course. His son and successor, Andronicos II, unlike his father, was opposed to the Latin rites and the Union, and helped the monks restore their properties. Unwittingly, however, Andronicos was to deal a near fatal blow to Athos. The Catalan mercenaries, whom he had hired to protect colonies in Asia Minor, became uncontrollable and were dismissed. They encamped on Kassandra, the westernmost of the three promontories of Chalkidiki, and from there, for two years, they plundered the Mountain, massacred monks, burned down monasteries and then departed, taking with them priceless treasures. Thus the number of monasteries was reduced to 25, of which 19 still survive.

Andronicos and successive Emperors of Constantinople and Trebizond helped to restore buildings and encourage monastic life. At the same period, the Serbian nation was at the height of its power. Many Serbian rulers sent generous donations to the Athos monasteries, and particularly to Chelandari whose monks were then, as they are now, their fellow-countrymen, while many new Serbian monks travelled to Athos. As happened earlier, many *kellia* were constructed as dependencies of the monasteries, while others were raised to the status of monasteries; several monasteries were also amalgamated.

Its calm restored, Athos enjoyed in the fifteenth century one of the most peaceful periods in its history. Its monks continued their fanatical resistance to any suggestion of Union of the East with the western half of Christendom, and took an active part in the struggle for Orthodoxy. Eventually, with the fall of Thessalonica (1430) and later of Constantinople (1453), Mount Athos passed under the Turkish yoke, along with the rest of the Greek people. In order to save Athos, the monks chose to have good relations with the Sultans. As soon as Murat II captured Salonica they offered him submission. In exchange for their capitulation Murat II recognised the properties of the monasteries, a recognition confirmed by Mohamet II, conqueror of Constantinople, So, up to a point, the independence of Mount Athos was secured by the sultans' firmans, which refer to the Mountain as 'the country in which day and night the name of the God is revered', and as 'a refuge for the needy and for travellers'. During this period a certain prosperity obtained, which lasted throughout the sixteenth century. An example of this is the foundation of the monastery of Stavronikita about the middle of the century, which completed the number of monasteries now in existence. Moreover, during these years, or to be more exact, after the subjugation of Serbia by the Turks, so many Serbs took refuge on the Mountain that sometimes one of their number was elected to the office of *Protos.*

However, the heavy taxation imposed by the Turks and the confiscation of estates brought about an economic crisis in the monasteries. The difficulties were in part overcome by the adoption of the idiorrhythmic life, which became widespread in the early eighteenth century. One might fairly say that monasticism in this form took root to lighten the economic difficulties on the Mountain. In such monasteries abbots were replaced by committees of monks, just as the *Protos* in Karyes was replaced by four overseers. But even so, the number of monks decreased further. This resulted in the depopulation of many monasteries and the adoption of sketal life. The *sketae* built at that time still exist and function as monastic dependencies.

Even in these lean times the Mountain was not left totally without protectors and benefactors. The Tsars of Russia, the rulers of Hungary and Moldo-Wallachia, many patriarchs and many a pious layman hastened to help it to some extent out of its difficulties. The names of such donors are rightly found amongst those of the founders and builders of each monastery, for it is to them that the monasteries owe much of the restoration work carried out during the Turkish rule. The monks were permitted by the countries mentioned above to take to their domains fragments of the True Cross and relics of the saints in order to organise processions and services for the purpose of collecting donations. This permission, as well as the gifts, whether of cash or of other kinds, given to the monks, was really a means of recognising their many services, especially to the rulers of Moldo-Wallachia, as secretaries, teachers and preachers. They were also an expression of gratitude for the miracles perfomed by the relics and icons brought from the Holy Mountain.

At this point we should stress the intellectual contribution of the Holy Mountain to the enlightenment of the enslaved Greek people throughout the Turkish Occupation. Particularly in the seventeenth and eighteenth centuries Athos became the educational centre of Greece and the home of scholars and wise men. From the Mountain came many men of high intellectual calibre to serve the Greek people as patriarchs, bishops, teachers and preachers. The times cried out for such men to encourage the Greeks, to help them remain true to their ancestral traditions and to strengthen their faith, thus preparing the rebirth of Hellenism. It was to this end that the Athonite Academy was founded close to the monastery of Vatopedi. The Academy attracted famous teachers, such as Eugenios Voulgaris, and produced such illustrious pupils as Athanasios Parios, Kosmas Aitolos, and Tzertzoulas. At the same time the monk Kosmas Lavriotis established a Greek printing press at Lavra. Up to its destruction shortly before the outbreak of the War of Independence, it contributed to the spread of books on Athos and among the enslaved Greek people.

The intellectual development of Mount Athos and its generally progressive course stopped with the outbreak of the Greek War of Independence in 1821.

The monasteries, which had given advice during its preparation now offered practical support. A large number of monks abandoned Athos, where a Turkish garrison was quartered. Some sought to avoid the atrocities of the Turkish soldiers, others felt it their duty to fight against them, casting aside the habit and taking up the sword to join combat alongside their fellow-countrymen. A decade later, when the struggle for independence had ended in victory, the survivors returned to start the re-building and the restoration of the monasteries. Thus Athos embarked upon a new period of development which continues to this day.

In the last century a marked inflow of monks from abroad – Bulgarians, Romanians and especially Russians – who harboured not the interests of Orthodoxy but more earthly motives, tried to internationalise Mount Athos, without success. The Athonite monks resisted proudly the various external pressures, remaining an integral part of the Greek State, and a mostly Greek-born community, where Greek was the chief language, as it had always been, notwithstanding the existence of monks of other nationalities.

MOUNT ATHOS TODAY

On Mount Athos today there are twenty inhabited monasteries. This number has been fixed by the constitutional charter of Mount Athos, and it is no longer possible to found other monasteries. The charter lays down that if the number of monks increases beyond the capacity of the monasteries, then monks are to be sent to live in *kellia* or *sketae*. Listed in hierarchical order the monasteries are: Great Lavra; Vatopedi; Iveron; Chelandari; Dionysiou; Koutloumousiou; Pantokrator; Xeropotamou; Zographou; Docheiariou; Karakalou; Philotheou; Simonopetra; Saint Paul; Stavronikita; Xenophontos; Gregoriou; Esphigmenou; Saint Panteleimon; Kastamonitou.

The monasteries are the rulers of all Athos, which has been divided into twenty corresponding districts. To the twenty monasteries belong also the monastic dwellings on the peninsula. Only Karyes, where the monasterial authorities have their seat, does not come under their control. Futhermore, the monasteries are described as self-governing. They owe no obedience whatsoever to any ecclesiastical authority. Even the jurisdiction of the ecumenical patriarchate over Athos is limited to issues which concern the spiritual life of the Athonite community.

All the Athonite monasteries, are referred to as royal, patriarchal and stavropegiac. They are royal institutions because they were founded by the authorisation of the chrysobull of a Byzantine emperor. They are designated as patriarchal because their foundation was confirmed by a *sigillion* or decree of a patriarch, when these houses recognised and accepted the spiritual guidance of a patriarch. And, lastly, they are named stavropegiac, for this title stresses that their foundations were consecrated by the planting of a patriarchal cross.

The way of life adopted in all the monasteries is now *coenobitic*. There were *idiorrhythmic* monasteries until 1992. The difference between them was that in the coenobitic monasteries, as the word denotes, everything is communal; shelter, work, food and prayer, whereas in idiorrhythmic houses, although shelter and prayer remained communal, work and food were regulated by the individual monk to his own taste.

Whether coenobitic or idiorrhythmic, the architecture of the monasteries is

4. The Russian skete of St Andrew (the 'serai'), a dependency of the monastery of Vatopedi.

the same. This is because all the monasteries were founded as coenobitic houses, and functioned as such for a long period of time. It was only long after their founding that the idiorrhythmic way of life was adopted by some, but even there, on the great feast days of the year, meals were eaten in common in the idiorrhythmic houses.

In the monasteries, which, as has been said, are all coenobitic, the legislative authority is vested in the assembly of elders *(gerontia),* which is composed of a limited number of monks. The executive authority is the abbot, who is also the spiritual father of the community. He is chosen for life by those monks who have completed six years after their tonsure. A small committee of two or three members, the abbot's council, assists the abbot in his duties. Its members, chosen from the *gerontia,* serve for one year. Life in a coenobitic house is more organised, the fasts more strictly observed and the monks – brothers working at regular duties assigned to them every year by the monastery – are without any personal property. The monastery takes care of all personal needs of the monks.

In those monasteries which were idiorrhythmic the legislative authority belonged to the council of superiors *(synaxis),* elected for life, and the executive to two or three trustees, who held office for a year and were elected from the *syn-*

5. Kavsokalyvia. Skete belonging to the monastery of Great Lavra. →

axis. The various duties necessary for the smooth-running of the monasteries were assigned to the monks by the trustees. To supplement the meagre salaries they were paid for these tasks, the monks were free to engage in other activities. Thus the individual was at liberty to regulate his own life, but this should not go beyond the limitations imposed on him by Athonite monasticism.

During the last twenty years there were seven idiorrythmic houses on Mount Athos: Great Lavra, Vatopedi, Iveron, Chelandari, Pantokrator, Xeropotamou and Docheiariou. According to the constitutional charter then in force, an idiorrhythmic house could become coenobitic if its brotherhood unanimously so wishes, but a coenobitic house may not change its status. It is worth pointing out that this major change over has now taken place in all seven monasteries, that of Pantokrator being the last.

There are other monastic establishments on Athos belonging to the twenty monasteries and functioning as their dependencies. These are the *skete*, the *kellion*, the *kathisma* and the *hesychasterion*.

Sketae: there are twelve *sketae* scattered over the peninsula. The *sketae*, like the monasteries until recently, are divided into coenobitic and idiorrhythmic. Their inhabitants are chiefly occupied in farming and handicraft making.

The coenobitic *sketae* are four in number: Prophet Elijah (Russian), which belongs to the monastery of Pantokrator; St John the Baptist (Romanian), dependent on Great Lavra; St Andrew or the Serai (Russian), under the monastery of Vatopedi, and of the Virgin surnamed Bogodoritsa (Bulgarian), belonging to the monastery of St Panteleimon. A *skete* is made up of a number of cells, looking much like a monastery, with a communal church in the centre of the courtyard. These *sketae* follow the same pattern of life as the coenobitic monasteries, and each of them is ruled by a prior *(dikaios)* whose office corresponds to that of an abbot.

The idiorrhythmic *sketae*, which represent the original form, are all Greek and eight in number. They are the Annunciation of the Blessed Virgin Mary or the Xenophonite Skete belonging to Xenophontos, the New Skete or the *skete* of the Tower and St Demetrios or *Lakkoskete*, both dependencies of St Paul's; St Anne's and *Kavsokalyvia*, properties of Great Lavra; St John the Baptist belonging to Iveron; St Panteleimon inhabited by monks of Koutloumousiou and the Vatopedian *skete* of St Demetrios. A *skete* is a loosely structured community consisting of a number of huts. Here too there is a church at the centre, the *kyriakon*, in which the Sunday liturgies are said. The daily offices are said in the individual *kalyvae* to each of which a chapel is attached. These communities are governed by a prior or *dikaios,* who is chosen on May 8th from the elders *(gerontes)* and who rules with the assistance of four counsellors. Two of these counsellors are chosen from the inhabitants of the *skete,* two from the parent monastery.

Kellion. The *kellion* is a spacious monastic dwelling, very much like a farmhouse, containing a small chapel. A small stretch of land surrounds it, which, of course, varies according to its wealth and size. The *kellion* is held by three or more monks under deed of trust from the parent monastery, and its monks are occupied in farming and similar activities.

Kalyve. The *kalyve* is a dwelling similar to a *kellion* but smaller. It also contains a chapel, but no land is attached to it. The monks there live like a family, much as in a *skete* or *kellion*, and they are occupied in handicrafts. Several such abodes grouped together give the impression of a community, but they share no common administration and there is no interdependency. Such groups of *kalyvae* are to be found in the area of Kapsala near Karyes, and on the south-west side of the peninsula – Little St Anne, Katounakia and St Basil's. A *kalyve* is similar to a cottage in a *skete*, but it is generally smaller.

Kathisma. A *kathisma* is an even smaller structure than the *kalyve*, usually found close to the parent monastery. Here one monk dwells alone, who, in return for a small payment for the dwelling, also has his food from the monastery.

Hesychasterion. A *hesychasterion* is a hermitage proper. It is to be found in some desolate spot, often in a cliff face. They abound at the southern extremity of the cape. Sometimes it is a small hut, but it is more often a cave, scarcely altered, which one might liken to an eagle's nest. To the *hesychasteria* retreat monks who seek the most harsh and austere asceticism.

Such hermitages make up the famous settlement at Karoulia, which lies beyond the *skete* of St Anne in the direction of Great Lavra. Ravines and precipitous cliffs separate these huts and caves, and access is only possible by steps, chains and tortuous paths.

The Government of Mount Athos

With only a few exeptions, the government of Mount Athos is based on the seven *Typika* issued from the first recognition of organised monasticism on the Mountain to the earliest years of the last century. The most important are those of 971/2, 1046, 1394 and 1810, to which we have already referred in the foregoing pages. Mount Athos is governed now in accordance with the provisions of the constitutional charter of 1924, which was ratified two years later in 1926 by legislative decree. This charter laid down that the legislative authority is to be exercised by the Holy Assembly, composed of twenty members, that is the abbot from each of the ruling monasteries. The Holy Assembly meets at Karyes twice a year to ratify canonical enactments covering the organisation, government and administration of the monastic life on Athos. In exceptional circumstances a double council, composed of forty members, is held. The administrative authority is exercised by the Holy Community, which again is made up of twenty members, one from each monastery. They are elected on January 1st and hold office for one year, during which time they live in Karyes. The executive authority is exercised by a separate committee of four overseers, the Holy *Epistasia*, a body composed according to the division of the monasteries into four groups of five, each group taking a turn for a year. Thus each monastery is represented on this committee once every five years. Although the members of the *Epistasia* are equal in status, the member from the senior monastery of the tetrad ranks as the chief monk and is called the *Protoepistates*, a compound derived from the old *Protos* and the newer *epistates*. The senior monasteries from which the *Protoepistates* is chosen are Great Lavra, Vatopedi, Iveron, Chelandari and Dionysiou. The monasteries choose their representative on the *Epistasia* on June 1st and his term of office lasts for one year. Finally, judicial authority is shared between different bodies on and outside the Mountain.

Karyes is also the seat of the civil governor, responsible to the Ministry of Foreign Affairs in Athens. His duty is the faithful execution of the constitutional charter and the general maintenance of law and order. He is assisted by a small number of administrators and police officials. Their presence ensures the unimpeded functioning of the system outlined in the constitutional charter. In accordance with this and with the present Greek Constitution, the Holy Mountain is an autonomous part of the Greek State.

6. The Holy Epistasia, the secretariat of the Holy Community, and two of the policemen ('seimenides') serving on Mount Athos.

The life of the monks on Athos

Midnight, the universally accepted beginning and end of the day, does not count on Athos as such. Here the Byzantine system, where the time is reckoned from sunset and thus shifts according to the season, is followed; the exception is Iveron where the Chaldaic system is adopted, according to which the day begins at sunrise.

The monastic day is divided into three parts of eight hours each; one is dedicated to prayer, one to work and the third to sleep.

Prayer

The prayer of the monks is divided into public and private. All the monks unite in communal worship, that is the saying of the various offices and services in the central church and smaller chapels. The most common services are Vespers, Compline, Midnight Mass, Matins and the Liturgy, which increase in elaborateness on feast days and especially on the vigils before festivals. Almost all the services are held at night when the rest of the world either revels or sleeps.

Private worship is based on the short prayer *'Kyrie Eleison'* (Lord Jesus Christ, have mercy on me). Rosaries are frequently employed to number the prayers. The monks of the Holy Mountain especially revere the Blessed Virgin Mary, who, as we have said earlier, is regarded as the Queen of Athos.

7. A monk banging the semantron in the courtyard of a monastery.

8. *A monk of Simonopetra striking the bells on one of the highest balconies of the monastery.*

9. *Festival procession of an icon in one of the monasteries.*

10 - 11 - 12. *Moments of work and prayer in the church.*

13. *Ploughing: one of the occupations of the monks.*

Work

Each of the Athonite monks, who today number 1700, works for his own monastery. Tasks are assigned to him by his superiors. Hence provision is made for the performance of worship, the safe-keeping of the treasures, the care of the brothers and pilgrims etc. It should be noted that the relatively small numbers of monks in the monasteries is totally disproportionate to the many duties required of them, and it is quite usual to find one monk performing two or more such tasks. Many monasteries are obliged to hire lay labourers to carry out many of the necessary jobs, especially the ones outside the monastery. Some of the tasks assigned only to monks are listed below. The *pyloros* or *portaris* is the monk responsible for the opening and closing of the main gate of the monastery. He has his quarters within the gate tower, and is required to check the credentials of visitors and to conduct them to the *archontaris*. The *archontaris* is the monk responsible for providing food and lodging for visitors. He is sometimes assisted by another monk, the *pararchontaris* or sub-guestmaster.

The *koudounokroustis* or *kabinaris* beats the wooden gong (*semantron*) to summon the monks to the various services and rings the bells on feast days. The *ecclesiastikos* or *ecclesiarchis* is responsible for the preparation of the church before the services. The *bemataris* is the custodian of the holy relics in the chancel, whose duty it is to show them to any visitor or pilgrim who requests to see them. The *typikaris* is the master of ceremonies in the church, indicating to the cantors the *troparia* and readings for the day. The *anagnostis* or *diavastis* is the reader of the lessons in the church and in the refectory. The *trapezar-*

14. Completing the decoration on a wooden flower-vase: another of the occupations of the monks.

15. Monks painting icons in one of the many ateliers of Mount Athos.

16. A monk on the sea-shore; he is beating an octopus.

is is responsible for the refectory and the preparation of the tables. The *magei-ras* is the cook in charge of the monastic kitchen. The *magipas* is the monastic baker. The *docheiaris* is in charge of the storerooms. The *nosokomos* is the monk in charge of the infirmary and is responsible for nursing the sick monks. The *gerokomos* is the monk entrusted with the care of those monks who are too old and frail to be left alone. The *bibliophylax* or *bibliothekarios* holds the keys of the library and is responsible for the care and safety of the books. The *skevo-phylax* or *thesavrophylax* is the monk responsible for the building containing the treasure of the monastery. Usually more than one monk is appointed, and each holds his own key. The *synodikaris* is the monk responsible for the care and maintenance of the room in which the superiors of the monastery hold their meetings. The *prosmonarios* is the monk appointed in monasteries which house a miracle-working icon of the Virgin Mary to take charge of both the icon and its chapel. He recites prayers to the Virgin, and accepts the oblations of pilgrims. The *bordonaris* or *chatlaris* oversees the stabling and feeding of the monastery's

17. Carrying mail and messages to a monastery.

livestock. The *arsanaris* is the monk originally of the port, and now responsible for goods brought in from outside to supply the monastery. He may live in a tower there, or may go to the harbour only when necessary.

Food

In general, the diet of the monks of Athos is very frugal and is based on bread, oil, wine, olives, vegetables and pulses. Meat is rarely eaten on the Mountain and in the monasteries is totally banned. The ascetics in Eremos make no provision for food, and have only what passers-by may leave them, usually dry rusks and olives.

The monks on Athos maintain the old tradition of hospitality to all visitors. Many pilgrims or workmen, especially in the summer months, find food and lodging in the monasteries, absolutely free of charge. The guest chambers are always open, and even a passer-by will be offered a glass of water together with the traditional ouzo, *loukoumi* and coffee.

18. Karyes, seen from above.

KARYES – THE PROTATON

In addition to the monastic dwellings discussed in the preceding section, there is the small town of Karyes, the capital of the monastic state.

Karyes' establishment resulted from the dispersal of the *'Kathedra of the Elders'* which obliged the *Protos* (Primate) to move his seat from the heights of Zygos further towards the centre of the peninsula into the area called Mesi. There he founded a new *lavra* (community), later named Karyes, which slowly acquired many rights, since for a long time its authority and precedence was recognised by all the monasteries and *lavras* of Athos. The organisation of Karyes, if we judge from its layout, closely resembles that of an idiorrhythmic *skete.*

The office of *Protos* certainly existed from very early on. The first *Typikon* (charter), granted by the Emperor John I Tzimisces (971/2), laid dowm the procedure for his election. The *Protos* was recognised as the ruler of the entire Athos peninsula. In reality, however, his authority was very limited. He could not make any decision on common matters without consulting the committee of abbots. The charter also reduced the meetings of the council from three to one, which was to be held on the feast of the Dormition of the Virgin. The *Protos* was to attend with three acolytes, instead of the two sought by St Athanasios and one by Paul Xeropotaminos, a distinction which clearly demonstrates how much more powerful the *lavra* of the Karyes was compared to the others on the Mountain.

The *Protos* was to be elected by the assembly of abbots. The candidate had to resign from all other offices before assuming the administration of Karyes, which henceforth would be his official seat and residence. The office was held for life. The power of the *Protos*, however, diminished in the course of the eleventh century as the number of monks increased at the three biggest monasteries of Great Lavra, Vatopedi and Iveron. The second *Typikon*, issued in 1046 by Constantine IX Monomachos, laid down that the *Protos* was to have authority only in minor matters, and even then only in consultation with five or ten monks. This charter also criticised the prevailing conditions at Karyes, condemning the numerous commercial transactions which turned the settlement into a trading centre.

Following the ravages of the Catalan mercenaries in the early fourteenth century, the *Protos* acted as a force for the re-organisation of monastic life on Athos. To this position the Patriarch Nephon appointed Theophanes, granting him various rights. These included the use of *epigonatia;* the authority to install abbots and to choose and ordain readers, sub-deacons, and confessors. All these rights were afterwards confirmed by the Emperor Andronicos II Paleologos in his chrysobull of 1313. He also recognised the *Protos* as the indisputable ruler of Mount Athos. Together with this concession went the re-definition of the conditions for his election. The election was to taken place at Karyes from amongst the representatives of the Holy Mountain, and was subject to confirmation by the Patriarch of Constantinople. Later, the third *Typikon* (1394) abolished the provisional influence of the bishop of Ierissos and strengthened even further the powers of the *Protos*. It also defined the boundaries of the Protaton as the *lavra* of Karyes had come to be known. Another clause stipulated that in the assemblies the *Protos* and the abbot of Great Lavra should hold episcopal staffs and sit next to one another, while the other abbots took places on either side of them.

Subsequently, chiefly from the end of the sixteenth century onwards, the Protaton lost much of its considerable property and retained only a few buildings which belonged to the monastic community, together with a few *kellia* which were later sold. The office of *Protos* was abolished. Some of its functions were taken over by four *epistates*, while the remaining duties were transferred to the bishop of Ierissos, who was henceforth given the title 'of Ierissos and Mount Athos'. He resumed an active role in the affairs of Mount Athos and participated in the assemblies at Karyes.

After some time, however, the institution of *Protos* was re-established. But he now ruled together with the *epistates* from one of the four groups of five monasteries into which the Athonite community had been divided. As before, his appointment was confirmed by the Patriarch and was tenable for life. The *Protos* acted as the custodian of the keys of the assembly chamber, but he did not hold the seal of the Community. This seal was broken into four parts, one part being held by each of the four *epistates*. Internal antagonisms, however, once more prevented the office of *Protos* from becoming firmly established.

We have said earlier that today almost all the buildings which exist at Karyes belong to the twenty monasteries, sold to them in 1661 because of the economic difficulties of the Protaton. Amongst the numerous *kellia*, many of which are frescoed, are included the *'konakia'* – the quarters of the representatives of nineteen monasteries; only the monastery of Koutloumousiou has no *'konaki'* here because of its proximity to Karyes. The settlement is made up of many *kelliotes*, engaged in different handiworks, lay-brothers serving as traders, labourers and muleteers, and employees of the civil services. Apart from a handful of buildings, the Community today owns only the quarters of the legislative assembly, housing also the administrative units of the monastic state, and the church of the Protaton

This church, so named after the office of *Protos*, is dedicated to the Dormition of the Blessed Virgin Mary. Erected when the prestige of this office was at its highest, before the time of St Athanasios the Athonite (probably in the first half of the tenth century), it is the oldest church on Athos. It differs from the others in plan and architectural type, and was restored in the reign of the Emperor Andronicos II Paleologos (1282-1328), when it assumed its present form.

It belongs to the type of three-aisled basilica with a rectangular ground plan and a raised roof bearing windows on each side over the nave. It terminates in three semi-circular apses at the east end. Inside, four buttress-like walls divide the church into a cross-shaped room in the centre and four corner sections. Thus we have here a combination of a cross-shaped ground-plan with roofing of the basilica type, a compound form resulting from the reconstruction of the church at some period. The roofs, the work of the Restoration Service in 1955,

19. The church of the Protaton seen from the east, showing the bell-tower. In the background is the headquarters of the Holy Community.

are of concrete, shaped to imitate wooden beams and are covered by Byzantine tiles.

The frescoes are of considerable interest. They are thought to be the work of the famous painter Manuel Panselinos, chief representative of the Macedonian School at the beginning of the fourteenth century. The marble *templon* (iconostasis) retains the style of earlier Byzantine *templa*. Dated to the tenth century, it was re-erected during the most recent consolidation works carried out by the Archaeological Service when the post-Byzantine carved wooden *templon* was removed. In the sanctuary the miracle-working icon of the Virgin, the *'Axion Esti'*, is preserved. According to tradition, it dates back to the tenth century.

The church has two narthexes: the western is dated to 1507, while the northern, dated to 1534, more closely resembles a stoa. A cenotaph stands here, commemorating the monks slain in the Catalan raids of the early fourteenth century when the original building was destroyed.

Behind the church to the east rises the bell tower, built by the *Protos* Serafim in the year 1534/5 and later repaired.

The library of the Protaton is housed in a secure room in the tower, and contains some 117 manuscripts, of which 47 are written on parchment, together with a significant number of printed books. Amongst the archives of the Protaton is the first *Typikon* of Mount Athos, referred to as *'Tragos'* (Billygoat) because it is written on goatskin.

The following chapters contain a brief description of each of the twenty monasteries, in hierarchical order.

THE TWENTY MONASTERIES OF MOUNT ATHOS

GREAT LAVRA

Great Lavra is the earliest and biggest foundation on Mount Athos. Built on a rocky outcrop where the peninsula ends, it stand where Mount Athos itself slopes gently down to the sea in green hillocks. It is about twenty minutes' walk from the shore, which is protected by its port-tower. Its feast day is the Dormition of St Athanasios the Athonite (July 5th).

It is variously referred to in old documents as 'Lavra of the Black Habit', 'Lavra of lord Athanasios', 'Lavra of St Athanasios', 'Great Lavra' and simply 'Lavra'. *Lavra* here means a monastery with a large number of monks.

The foundation of the monastery marks the change-over on Athos from the individual ascetic life to organised monasticism. Its founder was the learned monk Athanasios, an innovative figure in the Mountain's history. He had taken his vows at a monastery of Olympos in Bithynia when the abbot there was the renowned Michael Maleinos, uncle of the future Emperor Nicephoros Phocas. There Athanasios became the firm friend of Phocas, already commander of the East. It was Phocas who prevailed on Athanasios to leave Olympos for Athos with the promise that he would later join him in the eremetical life.

Though he may have had his reservatios in the beginning, Athanasios founded Lavra in 963, basing his hopes on his friend the emperor. He chose as its site the spot where probably the ancient Pelasgian city of Akrothoi had stood. According to his biography, written in the eleventh century, he first enclosed the site with a wall. He then constructed the *katholikon* (central church) within the enclosure, and lastly completed the rows of cells. This colossal work would never have started had it not been for funds sent by Nikephoros Phocas. Phocas, by this time emperor, and therefore unable to honour the promise he had given, tried to atone for this by financing the work. He also made special provision for the maintenance of the first eighty monks at Lavra. Furthermore he endowed the monastery with various properties and dependencies. One of these was the monastery of Peristeri near Salonica. He also presented Great Lavra with gifts of relics, including fragments of the True Cross, and many works of art.

20. Great Lavra. Part of the interior of the monastery.

John Tzimisces, successor of Phocas, with whom Athanasios maintained friendly relations, continued to give financial support. He doubled the annual provision for the needs of the newly formed monastery. This helped to complete the building of Lavra, which became the core and model of a new form of monastic life on Athos.

Thanks to the generosity of successive emperors, the monastery prospered from its nearly days. The number of monks rapidly increased and soon exceeded the original eighty. The coenobitic way of life took firm root not only at Lavra, but throughout Mount Athos. In particular the monastery received considerable assistance from Basil II. In addition to confirming the monastery's right to the island of St Eustratios, this emperor gave it property elsewhere and numerous other gifts.

Athanasios, who lived until the end of the tenth century, was succeeded as abbot of Lavra by Eustratios, whose signature we find on a document of 1016.

Great Lavra, in common with all Athonite monasteries, experienced many fluctuations in fortune. At some periods it flourished, at others it declined, and there was even a period when it was virtually deserted. From the middle of the eleventh, when it numbered about seven hundred monks, until the early fourteenth century, Lavra prospered. Thereafter, following the destruction wrought by various pirate raiders, there was a noticeable slackening in the application of the precepts of St Athanasios and a deviation from the tenets of coenobitic monasticism. Numbers started to dwindle and by the early sixteenth century were dangerously low. The result of this depressed condition of the monastery was that it changed from the coenobitic to the idiorrhythmic way of life. The experiment, however, was short-lived, and Lavra reverted to the coenobitic life thanks to the efforts of the Patriarch of Alexandria, Silvester, and the Holy Assembly (1574). Nevertheless, the decline continued, and by the beginning of the seventeenth century the monastery had only five or six monks. Its economic position remained desperate until 1655, when Patriarch Dionysios III came and bequeathed all his property to Lavra.

Subsequently, the monastery once more became idiorrhythmic. From the middle of the eighteenth century (1744), when the Patriarch Paisios II confirmed certain of its old privileges, its history reveals no startling reversals.

Apart from the help afforded by the patriarchs mentioned above, Lavra received assistance in many ways from the rulers of the countries of the Danube basin and from the Tsars of Russia throughout the years of the Ottoman Occupation.

The several-storeyed buildings of the monastery enclose a quadrangle which, seen from the outside, much resembles a small embattled town. The *katholikon*, several small chapels, the refectory and some other buildings stand in the court. At the south-west corner of the precint stands the ancient and imposing tower of Tzimisces, which dominates the monastery.

In front of the main entrance to the monastery is a portico resting on four columns. In addition to this main gateway there is a smaller entrance in the southern side. Many of the buildings, even whole wings, have been renewed in comparatively recent years. Thus the south range dates from 1769, and the east from 1862.

The **katholikon** of Great Lavra was the earliest to be built on the Mountain, and it has served as a model for all the *katholika* in the Athonite monasteries. It is a composite four-columned Byzantine church, with two apses, two side chapels on either side of the *lite* and a double narthex, that is a *lite* (eso-

21. General view of the interior of Great Lavra, showing the tower of Tzimisces in the background.

narthex) and exo-narthex. The church stands approximately in the centre of the large court. It was originally dedicated to the Annunciation of the Blessed Virgin Mary, but was re-consecrated to the Dormition of St Athanasios the Athonite, probably in the fifteenth century.

The murals of the church were executed by the famous Cretan painter Theophanes in 1535 and are considered the best work of his mature period. These frescoes are amongst the most magnificent on Athos. The two narthexes were decorated with frescoes much later, in 1854, at the expense of the archimandrite Benjamin.

Left and right of the eso-narthex are two side chapels, one dedicated to St Nicholas and the other to the Forty Martyrs. The former has frescoes, painted in 1560 by Frangos Katellanos, a contemporary, and maybe even a pupil of the great Cretan painters. His art, however, differs markedly from that of the Cretan School.

In the Chapel of the Forty Martyrs is the tomb of Athanasios enclosing his remains. Its cloth covering bears a picture of the saint. The same chapel houses two notable portable icons, one of Christ, the other of the Virgin surnamed *Oikonomissa* (Stewardess). The sixteenth-century wall-paintings were retouched in 1854.

In addition to these two side-chapels of the *katholikon*, Great Lavra con-

22. The façade and entrance to the refectory of Great Lavra.

tains a further fifteen chapels within its bounds, one of which, St George, is frescoed. Of the others, the most important are the chapel of St Athanasios, next to the treasury where his heavy iron cross and staff are preserved, and the chapel of the Virgin *Koukouzelissa* with its eponymous icon of the Virgin. Nineteen other chapels outside the monastery precinct belong to Great Lavra. Its dependencies consist of five *kathismata*, forty *kellia* in the settlements at Kerasia, Morphonou, Provata and Karyes.

Outside the main entrance to the church stands the **phiale** - the basin for the blessing of the holy water. This *phiale* is the biggest on Athos. Its dome is supported by eight columns, and the low circular wall at its base contains carved marble panels of Byzantine relief work. Inside, the cupola is decorated with post-Byzantine painted representations of scenes connected with the blessing of the waters. It is shaded by a cypress tree, said to be a thousand years old and supposedly planted by St Athanasios.

Further west, and immediately opposite the entrance to the *katholikon*, stands the **refectory**. This too has been decorated with striking murals by Cre-

23. Inside Great Lavra with part of the court of the monastery.

tan painters. Of the scenes, the most noteworthy are the Last Supper, the Heavenly Ladder, the Second Coming, the Tree of Jesse and the twenty-four strophes of the *Akathistos* Hymn. There are also scenes from the life of the Virgin and from the lives of many ascetics and saints. Lastly, a series of portraits of ancient Greek philosophers and writers are to be seen there: they are those of Philon, Solon, Pythagoras, Socrates, Aristotle, Thales, Galen, Plato and Plutarch.

The **treasury** of the monastery is very rich. It is housed in a free-standing building behind the church on the eastern side of the court. Amongst its many treasures the most magnificent are the crown and so-called *sakkos* of Nikephoros Phocas, an old quiver, coverings for printed Gospels, sacerdotal vestments, ecclesiastical plate, crosses, pectorals, chalices, valuable portable icons and many other objects. In the church are displayed fragments of the True Cross and the relics of many saints.

The **library**, housed next to the treasury and in the same building, is considered the wealthiest on Mount Athos. It contains 2500 manuscripts, of which

24. One of the many dependencies of Great Lavra: the skete of St Anne.

470, as well as 50 liturgical scrolls, are written on parchment. Some of these, such as A76, A86, A111, Ω75 and the so-called Phocas Gospel in the sacristy, are richly illuminated. Another section of the library contains over 20,000 printed volumes, amongst which are many notable incunabula and old books.

Since its foundation Great Lavra has always ranked as the first monastery in the hierarchy of Mount Athos. It follows the coenobitic way of life, and at the present moment numbers 420 monks, of whom 50 live in the monastery and 370 are divided between its various dependencies.

To Great Lavra belong three **sketae:** St Anne, Kavsokalyvia and Prodromos, as well as the dwellings at Eremos, namely St Basil's, Little St Anne's, Katounakia and Karoulia. All these are sited on the south-west side of the peninsula, beyond the monastery of St Paul and the New Skete as one heads towards Great Lavra.

St Anne's is a Greek idiorrhythmic *skete*, the biggest and the oldest on the Mountain. It is built on a richly vegetated hillside plentifully supplied with springs on the west coast of Mt Athos. It lies immediately beyond the New Skete a little before arriving at Eremos. Hermits had settled here earlier, but the importance of this *skete* increased during the seventeenth century. Today it has fifty-one *kalyvae*, not all inhabited, and the *kyriakon* (church), which was built between 1752-55 and frescoed in 1757. The left foot of St Anne, the mother of the Virgin, is preserved here. The *skete* boasts a relatively good library with about one hundred manuscripts, which for the most part are of recent date and are written on paper.

Kavsokalyvia is a Greek idiorrhythmic *skete* consisting of forty *kalyvae*, of which some lack chapels and most are today uninhabited. It is sited beyond

25. The dread Karoulia with some of the kalyves – the 'eagles' eyries'.

Eremos in the direction of Great Lavra, on cliffs above the sea. It acquired its name from the activities of a hermit, Maximos, who built a hut here in the fourteenth century, which he burnt every time he saw others preparing to live too close to him, replacing it with another higher up the slopes. The present church was built in 1745, its narthex was added in 1804, and it was frescoed in 1820. There are about fifty modern paper manuscripts in the library.

Prodromos: the Greek *kellion* of St John the Baptist was sold in the middle of the nineteenth century to two Moldavian monks. In 1857 it was raised to the status of a *skete* and was gradually recognised as Romanian because of the nationality of the monks living there. It lies between Kavsokalyvia and Lavra, and is built on the top of a low hill some 250 m. above the sea. Seen from afar it gives the impression of a strong rectangular building complex. The *kyriakon* stands in the centre of the court and was dedicated in 1866 to St John the Baptist. Some ten Romanian monks follow the coenobitic way of life here.

Eremos lies beyond the *skete* of St Anne's, on the lower slopes of Mount Athos. It comprises the settlements of Kerasia, St Basil's, Katounakia and the awe-inspiring Karoulia. These settlements are completely independent units, without any connection existing between them. This is partly because the terrain here is very wild, with sheer cliffs, and it is difficult to approach the isolated huts of these settlements. The ascetics and hermits who live here are absorbed day and night in prayer and spiritual exercises. Entirely beyond any connection with the world, they are heedless of bodily needs. They sing and praise the Lord continuously for His creation of the world, entreating Him ceaselessly for their own salvation and for that of all mankind.

41

THE MONASTERY OF VATOPEDI

Vatopedi, one of the larger monasteries, stands on what was probably the site of an ancient town, Dion. It is built above a small inlet on the north-east side of the peninsula, at the top of a green slope. The monastery is dedicated to the Annunciation of the Blessed Virgin Mary (March 25th).

The date of its foundation and the origin of its name still puzzle scholars. According to tradition, Vatopedi, was founded at the end of the fourth century by the Emperor Theodosius I, out of gratitude to the Virgin who saved his young son, Arcadius, shipwrecked off the shores of the Holy Mountain. The child was miraculously brought safely to shore close to a bramble bush, from which the monastery took its name (*vato*=bramble bush, *paedion*=child). We, however, believe that the alternative derivation of the name is more probable, namely that the monastery was so-called from the brambles which flourish round the monastery (*vato*=bush, *pedion*=field).

In old documents the monastery is referred to as the '*lavra* of Vatopedi' or the 'big monastery of Vatopedi'.

Historically, however, the founding of the monastery is to be placed in the second half of the tenth century. It was founded by three monks from Adrianopolis, Athanasios, Nicholas and Antonios. These three men came to Athos with the intention of living close to St Athanasios. After a while, however, he sent them to the area occupied by the present-day monastery where it seems that much earlier many hermits had lived. Perhaps there still existed one or more *kellia* which the brothers joined together to form the core of the new foundation.

Vatopedi is not mentioned in the first *Typikon* of Mount Athos (972), but amongst the co-signatories of an Act of the *Protos* Thomas, dated to 985, is its abbot, Nicholas. So, with some degree of certainty, we may assume that the present monastery was founded between 972 and 985.

Within a century, according to the evidence of the second *Typikon* (1046), Vatopedi ranked second in the hierarchy, as it still does today. It had a large number of monks, considerable wealth and many privileges. Amongst the latter for a time was its abbot's right to attend the councils at Karyes together

26. View of the sprawling monastery of Vatopedi from the sea.

27. Inside the monastery of Vatopedi, showing the katholikon, the refectory and the bell-tower.

with four attendants. Vatopedi received much assistance from members of the Comnenos family, especially from Manuel I, as is evident from his chrysobull. At the same period nine smaller monasteries became its dependencies; Ieropatoros, Verroitou, Kalentzi, St Demetrios, Xystrou, Tripolitou, Chalkeos, Trochala and Philadelphou.

Before the close of the twelfth century two eminent Serbians, father and son, known as Symeon and Savvas, came to dwell as monks at Vatopedi. To them Vatopedi granted the cell of Chelandari, in the region Milea, which they soon enlarged to form an independent monastery. This is the reason for the close relationship which is still maintained. Hence the monks of Vatopedi officiate at the feast day services at Chelandari, and monks from Chelandari do likewise at Vatopedi. Moreover, the *proistamenos* of either monastery, sent on such occasions to the other, receives at the entrance to the host monastery its abbatial staff and pectoral cross.

Vatopedi suffered from the raids of pirates, of the Unionists and finally of the Catalan mercenaries, and began to decline. The Paleologue Emperors made gifts to the monastery to help its recovery, especially Andronicos II in his chrysobull of 1292. It also received assistance from the Commander-in-Chief, Demetrios Paleologos, and from many Serb rulers. In the same period the monastery became the home of many illustrious men, including Gregory Palamas, later archbishop of Salonica, Maximos Trivolis or the Greek, the great apostle of the Russians, the Patriarch Gennadios after his abdication from the ecumenical throne, and many others.

28. *South side of the katholikon of the monastery of Vatopedi.*

But Vatopedi's prosperity lasted only for a time. The monastery slipped once more into decline. Maximos the Greek himself described it as a *lavra*, and tells us that in his time a semi-coenobitic form of life was observed. Thus about 1541 here too the idiorrhythmic way of life was introduced, which had already been adopted by some other monasteries on Athos. In 1575, however, the monastery reverted to the coenobitic form, as a result of the efforts of the Patriarch of Alexandria, Silvester. Later, it turned once again to the idiorrhythmic life, which it followed until 1989 when, once again, it became coenobitic.

Heavy taxation imposed by the Turks in the seventeenth century forced Vatopedi to sell many of its estates to meet diverse needs and to support its monks, who at that time numbered three hundred. To overcome these difficulties Vatopedi was assisted by the Tsars of Russia and the rulers of the Danubian principalities, who contributed open-handedly. Nevertheless, the monastery was able to regain financial stability only for a very short time.

It was in the eighteenth century that Vatopedi came once more to know prosperity. This new acme can also be deduced from the fact that the Athonite Theological Academy functioned with monies supplied by Vatopedi. The Academy was housed in a separate building close to the monastery. Many of the conventual buildings were renovated at this period, and the monastery increased in size with the addition of new buildings. The most generous donors were the Patriarchs Kyprianos of Constantinople and Gerasimos of Alexandria, but there were many other contributors, monks and laymen, mostly anonymous, from the enslaved Greek nation.

Some of the buildings visible today date from the founding. Many have undergone extensive restoration made necessary as the result of destruction either by pirate attacks or by fire. Other buildings have been altered to provide the space necessary to accommodate ever-increasing numbers of recruits. The buildings enclose a very large paved courtyard of roughly polygonal shape whose northern side, which runs parallel to the sea, is 200 metres long. The whole impression is that of a fortress.

The **katholikon** was built in the tenth century, and is dedicated to the Annunciation of the Blessed Virgin Mary. Its plan, with certain later changes and additions, is that common to all monasteries on Athos, which we described at Great Lavra. Of more recent date is the exo-narthex and the bell-tower. The exo-narthex, constructed in 1426, is a two-storey building with an open arcade on the ground floor. The tower which abuts it was built in 1427. The present wooden *templon* was carved in 1788. In the chapel of St Nicholas part of the low marble iconostasis of Byzantine date is preserved.

The frescoes of the *katholikon*, according to one inscription, were executed at the beginning of the fourteenth century in the reign of the Emperor Andronicos II and the rule of the hieromonach Arsenios. Unfortunately, the earliest paintings have been retouched twice (1739 and 1819), which has somewhat diminished their original value. Nevertheless, one may discern under the weak colours of the repainting the characteristics of the Macedonian School, especially in representations of the Last Supper, the Betrayal, the Passion of Christ and others. The paintings of the exo-narthex, which are more recent than those described above, were also retouched in 1819.

In the church are some fine Byzantine mosaics, the only example of such work on Mount Athos. Amongst the scenes represented are the Annunciation of the Virgin, above the capitals of the two eastern columns of the nave; the Deesis, in the tympanum of the entrance to the eso-narthex; and, for a second time, the Annunciation below it. The representation of St Nicholas occupies the space over the entrance to the eponymous side chapel. We should also mention the magnificent marble *opus sectile* floor.

A large number of smaller chapels in addition to the katholikon lie within the boundaries of the monastery. Five are within the katholikon: those of St Nicholas and of St Demetrios lie left and right of the eso-narthex; that of the Virgin of Consolation is roughly above the latter, while those of the Archangels and of the Holy Trinity are right and left of the galleries. The ceremony of tonsuring the novices is performed in the chapel of the Virgin of Consolation, built and frescoed in 1678 at the expense of Gregory of Laodicea. The frescoes were retouched in 1846.

Outside the church, in the courtyard, there are two other chapels; that of the Holy Girdle, so-called from the part of the belt of the Virgin nowadays kept in the sanctuary of the *katholikon*, and that of Sts Cosmas and Damian. These, like the chapels mentioned above, are decorated with hagiographical scenes.

Twelve other chapels are to be found incorporated within the ranges of cells. Only one, that of St Andrew, is frescoed.

Finally, outside the precinct, there are other chapels, including that of the Holy Apostles in the cemetery, quite recent; that of St Nicholas; that of All Saints in the vineyard, now in ruins; that of St Modestus with frescoes.

Outside the main entrance to the *katholikon* and close to the façade, stands the **phiale**, and opposite stands the refectory, built during the reign of the Em-

29. *Another view of the spacious courtyard of Vatopedi.*

peror Alexios in the twelfth century. It was frescoed much later, in 1786.

Vatopedi has been presented with many gifts and consequently has one of the most valuable **treasuries** on the Holy Mountain. Here are kept many rare objects of immense value; portable icons of the Crucifixion and of St Anne, a portable icon of St George made of agate, gold-embroidered vestments, ecclesiastical plate, manuscripts of the Gospels and a large selection of rarities. In the sanctuary of the *katholikon* fragments of the True Cross are preserved, together with relics of saints, two miniature icons, that is to say, a diptych of Christ and the Virgin known as the *'Ninia of Theodora'*, a part of the reed on which the sponge of vinegar was offered to Christ on the Cross, and many other relics.

On the lower floor of the high tower are many other works of art amongst which is a multi-coloured cup, the jasper, gift of Manuel Paleologos. Also here is the archive room of the monastery which contains precious chrysobulls, kerobulls and other documents relating to the history of the monastery and dating mostly from the fourteenth century. A large part of the early archive was probably destroyed in the Catalan raids.

The Virgin's girdle, mentioned above, was first known to have been in the monastery of Vlachernae in Constantinople, and later in Hagia Sophia. From there it came into the possession of the King of Serbia, Lazaros I, who later presented it to Vatopedi.

Lastly, in many different corners of the monastery, are numerous portable icons, of which we make special mention of those of the Virgin variously surnamed; *Paramythia* (she who consoles), *Antiphonetria* (she who retorts), *Esphagmene* (she who was wounded), *Elaiovrytis* (she who flows with oil), *Ktitorissa* (the founder), and *Vematarissa* (the sacristan). Each of these icons is connected with an episode in the history of the monastery.

The **library** is rich both in manuscripts and in printed books. There are more than 2000 manuscripts, of which 625, as well as 25 liturgical scrolls in the archives, are written on parchment. From the illuminated manuscripts we would select for special mention numbers 602, 609, 655 and 1199, with their fascinating miniatures and other decorations. The printed books number more than 25,000 volumes, and include many old and valuable editions.

The library is temporarily housed in a tower at the north-east corner of the courtyard. Both for the library and for the treasury, at the moment next to the refectory in a free-standing building, new homes are being prepared in the present rebuilding of the north wing, to which they will soon be transferred.

To Vatopedi belongs the Greek **skete of St Demetrios**, half an hour's walk or so towards the mountain. It is probably on the site of the older monastery, Chalkeos. Although it consists of twenty-one *kalyvae*, most are boarded up and only three or four monks observe the idiorrhythmic way of life here. Its *kyriakon* was frescoed in 1755, and the exo-narthex, constructed in 1796, in 1806. The library contains 73 manuscripts – recently transferred to the monastery – and about 200 printed books.

Vatopedi also owns the large Russian **skete of St Andrew** or the **Serai**, on the site of the older Xystrou monastery, near Karyes. This *skete*, was still a *kellion* dedicated to St Antony, when the Patriarchs of Constantinople Seraphim II and Athanasios III rebuilt it and gave it its present name in 1763. In 1842 it was given by Vatopedi to Bessarion and other Russian monks who, after many efforts, turned the *kellion* into a coenobitic *skete*. This change in status was ratified by a decree of the Patriarch Anthimos IV in 1849. Shortly afterwards, between 1857 and 1900, the *skete* was enlarged by the addition of big and imposing buildings forming a quadrangle. Today the *skete* is deserted, only one wing being occupied by the school of Athonis. Its impressive *kyriakon*, whose intermittent building lasted more than twenty years between 1867 and 1900, survives intact. It is reckoned to be the biggest church on Mount Athos and amongst the most magnificent in the East. In addition to the *kyriakon* there are other chapels there. That of St Antony, which served as the original *kyriakon*, has frescoes of 1766.

Lastly, the monastery has twenty-seven *kellia;* twenty-two of them are in the settlement of Kolitsou and its environs, (only a few are inhabited), as well as west of the monastery, and five are in Karyes. One of the latter, that of the Ascension, is used as the monastery's headquarters at Karyes. The monastery also owns ten *kalyvae*, all in ruins, at Kalamitsi, and some *metochia* (properties) outside the Holy Mountain, at Porto Lago, on Samos and elsewhere.

Vatopedi at present numbers about seventy monks who live in the monastery and its dependencies.

30. The phiale and the clock with the 'negro' on the façade of the katholikon.

31. View of the monastery of Iveron from the sea.

THE MONASTERY OF IVERON

The monastery of Iveron is dedicated to the memory of the Dormition of the Blessed Virgin Mary. Situated above a picturesque inlet on the north-east side of the peninsula, close to a gushing stream of water, it is reached after half an hour's easy downhill walk from Karyes.

The monastery was founded in the last quarter of the tenth century, only a little later than those of Great Lavra and Vatopedi. It stands on, or close to, the site of the earlier *lavra* of St Clement. With its foundation are linked the names of John the Iberian and John Tornikios. More probably, however, these two names represent only one person, although Georgian sources lead us to believe otherwise. John Tornikios, who was a courtier of David, ruler of Iberia (Georgia), and a Byzantine dignitary, rejected all his worldly honours in order to become a monk. He took his vows at a monastery somewhere in Macedonia, and later went to Olympos. From there he journeyed to Athos, where he settled in an isolated spot in the vicinity of Lavra. There he had the opportunity to know Athanasios, and to stay close by his side as his disciple. For a short time he practised the monastic life here with his own son Euthymios and his nephew George.

The Emperor Basil II summoned the monk Tornikios to the capital, to draw on his skill to settle assorted diplomatic and military questions, and, more particularly, his help to suppress the revolt of the general Bardas Skleros, the leader of an insurrection against the emperor. Tornikios, obeying the imperial command, put aside the habit, and together with the ruler David, set out to fight Bardas, whose rebellion he successfully quelled. Tornikios then returned to the Mountain, and started to build the present monastery, or, more accurately, to enlarge and renew the already existing buildings of the *lavra* of St Clement. This extensive undertaking was started and completed through the generous gifts of the emperor and through Tornikios's own spoils of war.

From the first the new monastery was called Iveron (of the Iberians) because of the origin of the founders and of the first monks to reside there, and this name has been preserved to this day. However, in 1357 a decree of the Patriarch Kallistos turned this Georgian house over to the Greek monks, who by then exceeded the Iberians in number.

From its earliest days up until the fourteenth century, the newly founded monastery added to its domain many smaller houses, including that of Leontios in Salonica, that of John of Kolobos at Ierissos, of St Savva, of Chaldos, of Kapsakos and of many others. Of course Iveron did not remain untouched by the successive raids against the Mountain or by their inevitable consequences.

Particularly devastating were the incursions of pirates, the armies of the Unionists and, in the early fourteenth century, the Catalan mercenaries. After the latter, the Paleologue Emperors, the ruler of Serbia, Stephen IV Dusan, and especially Gorgoranis, ruler of Georgia, and his heirs, all contributed to the cost of restoring the monastery.

The house enjoyed a new period of prosperity which lasted until the end of the sixteenth century, when grave economic difficulties were experienced. The position was so serious that, seeking a solution to their problem, the Iberians returned to their country and surrendering the keys of the monastery to the ruler, Alexander VI, begged him to provide financial support. They visited neighbouring countries also, and the result of their missions was the amassing of vast sums of money which enabled them not only to clear the debts of the monastery, but also to erect new buildings. The number of monks increased, and in a short time had risen significantly.

In the middle of the seventeenth century Iberian monks, acceding to the request of the Tsar Alexios, visited Russia, taking with them as a gift a copy of the icon of the Virgin *Portaitissa* (of the gate), by means of which the Tsar's ailing daughter was cured. Instead of giving the monks money, Alexios, out of gratitude both to the monks and to the Virgin, gave them the wealthy monastery of St Nicholas in the centre of Moscow.

32. View of the monastery of Iveron from the south-east.

Many patriarchs also took to heart the welfare of Iveron and did their best to help it in different ways. Thus, in 1622, Cyril I confirmed by a decree his gifts of the Comitissa to the monastery, and Cyril II, in 1635, by another decree confirmed Iveron's rights over the monastery of Vlatadon in Salonica. Further, Parthenios conferred the titles patriarchal and stavropegiac in 1675, and in 1678 Dionysios IV presented his library. The monastery was also favoured by later ecumenical Patriarchs, including Seraphim I, Ioannikios III, Neophytos VIII and Kallinikos IV. For a short time Gregorios V, martyred at the start of the War of Independence, resided here.

After the Greek War of Independence (1821) Iveron found itself again in economic difficulties, largely because of the substantial contribution it had made to the common struggle. These difficulties were exacerbated by two extensive fires which destroyed one wing of the monastery (1845 and 1865). This wing has since been rebuilt with monies given by the faithful.

The **katholikon** of the monastery is dedicated to the Dormition of the Blessed Virgin Mary. Restored in 1513, it was originally built in the first half of the eleventh century by the Iberian monk George Varasvatzes, who for many years held the office of abbot. It stands almost in the centre of the court and follows the typical plan of the Byzantine Athonite church. The magnificent marble *opus sectile* floor with various geometrical patterns and bearing the inscription in capital letters 'I erected these columns and they shall not be shak-

33. The katholikon and the phiale of the monastery.

en by time. George the Iberian, monk and founder' has been preserved. Also worthy of notice are the reused bizonal capitals decorated with acanthus leaves and rams' heads which top the columns of the nave.

The wall-paintings belong to different periods between the sixteenth and the nineteenth century, when they were repainted. Of interest also is the post-Byzantine wood iconostasis carved with rich foliage; the finely carved door made of silver and ebony, which leads from the exo-narthex to the inner narthex; and the seven-branched silver lampstand in the shape of a lemon tree with thirty gilded lemons. According to the metrical inscription in Russian and Greek, it was presented to the archimandrite Cyril by the inhabitants of Moscow in 1818 as a gift for his monastery.

A third, glazed narthex, decorated with wall-paintings, was added to the double narthex in 1795.

In front of the church stands the **phiale** for the blessing of the waters, reconstructed after the fire of 1865. Opposite the west door of the church is the refectory, which was rebuilt and enlarged by the archimandrite Athanasios the Akarna in 1848. The tall bell tower above its entrance was constructed in the same year.

Opposite the main entrance, and roughly in the centre of the south wing, rises the defence tower of the monastery, built in 1725. It is today in very ruinous condition, in contrast to the fine, older (1626) port tower close to the sea.

In addition to the *katholikon* there are sixteen small chapels within the monastery enclosure. Of these, two are frescoed; that of St Nicholas (1846) and that of the Archangels (1812), which are to the right and left of the inner narthex. In the latter, relics of some one hundred and fifty saints are preserved, together with parts of the instruments of Our Lord's Passion and a fragment of the True Cross.

The courtyard contains two other noteworthy chapels; that of the Virgin *Portaitissa* and that of St John the Baptist. The former, close to the original entrance to the monastery and dated to 1680, houses the miracle-working icon of the Virgin *(Portaitissa)* enclosed in a gilt covering. The story goes that the icon, travelling over the sea from Constantinople, came to land at a spot near the present monastery. The paintings of the chapel were executed in 1683, and the iconostasis was carved in 1785. In the narthex, frescoed in 1774, between the representations of the saints are also eminent figures of ancient Greece; the law-giver Solon, the writers Sophocles, Thucydides and Plutarch, the philosophers Plato and Aristotle and the Kings Alexander and Darius.

The other chapel, of St John the Baptist, lies to the east of the former. It was re-built from the foundations by the abbot Agapios in 1710, and frescoed a little later in 1714. Its iconostasis (1711) is a brilliant example of the wood-carver's art. The remaining twelve chapels house only portable icons.

Outside the monastery are eleven *kathismata*, thirteen *kellia* in the direction of Karyes, another three towards Philotheou and ten more in or near Karyes. Of these, that of St Demetrios is used today as the quarters for the monastery's representative at Karyes. The monastery also holds several properties *(metochia)* beyond the bounds of the Mountain, for example on Samothrace.

To the monastery of Iveron belongs the **skete** of **St John the Baptist**, or the **Iberian skete**, which is found to the west of the monastery about half an hour's walk towards the mountain. It is a Greek idiorrhythmic *skete* founded in 1730, although the *kyriakon* dates only from 1779, with frescoes of 1799. The *skete* today consists of eight *kalyvae* where only five or six monks dwell.

34. The holy spring on the shore near the monastery of Iveron.

The **treasury** of Iveron contains one of the richest and most valuable collections on Athos. It is housed alongside the library in a new one-storey building in the court. Its treasures are of inestimable value, and include gold-embroidered sacerdotal vestments, ecclesiastical plate, crosses, communion chalices, pectorals, mitres, the complete sacerdotal dress of the Patriarch Dionysios IV, the cloak of Gregory V, a finely embroidered curtain of the Royal Door, the work of the embroideress Kokkona Orologa, representing the Assumption (*Metastasis*) of the Virgin Mary, and many other sacred objects and relics. Finally, the so-called *sakkos* of the Emperor John Tzimisces is displayed in a case in the library. This liturgical vestment is decorated with various arabesque patterns and bears representations of ten lions' heads and four two-headed eagles. It is probably a sacerdotal vestment of the fifteenth century.

The **library** is richly stocked and well-organised. It contains more than 2000 manuscripts, varying widely in content and made of different materials, and 15 liturgical scrolls. Of these codices, 123 are written on parchment, another 23 on bombasine or paper. To these must be added about 100 parchment texts in the Georgian language. The illustrations in several of the Greek manuscripts (nos. 1, 5, 55, 56, 111, 463, 874, etc.) are of interest. In addition to its manuscripts the library contains over 20,000 printed books, amongst which are some very fine first editions and incunabula.

The library also contains several important imperial and patriarchal documents, the most noteworthy of which are the chrysobulls of the Emperors, Constantine VII Porphyrogennitos (946 and 958), Romanos II (960) and Basil II.

The monastery of Iveron occupies the third rank in the hierarchical order of the twenty Athonite monasteries. It is coenobitic (1990), and, as we noted above, since the beginning, has been peopled by monks from Iberia, for which country it has always been an important spiritual centre. The last Iberian monk there died in 1955. Today, about ninety monks dwell in the monastery, its *skete* and the different *kellia*.

THE MONASTERY OF CHELANDARI

Chelandari, dedicated to the Presentation of the Mother of God, (feast day November 21st) lies on the north-east side of the peninsula and is the most northerly of the Athonite monasteries. Although only half an hour's walk from the sea, where its port-tower stands, Chelandari remains unseen from its harbour, closed in by low, thickly-wooded hills.

In all probability the name of the monastery is derived from the founder of an earlier monastic settlement at this spot, who was called Chalendaris. The name occurs in a document of the tenth century: 'We wrote through George called Chelandari'. Later, in a document of 1141, preserved at Lavra, we find amongst the other signatories a monk by the name of Symeon (?) of the monastery of Chelandari. The view that the monastery is so-named because its plan resembles the outlines of the Byzantine ship known as the *chelandion* does not seem very plausible.

Many scholars, however, refer to the monastery as Chiliantari. The etymology of the spelling is based on *'chilioi'* and *'antara'* (a thousand mists), because 'mist pours over the site'. Others spell the name Chiliandari or Chilandari, a derivate from *'chilioi'* and *'andres'* (a thousand men). This is a reference to the tradition of the thousand pirates who had planned to pillage the monastery. To carry out their attack they had divided into two bands which, unable to distinguish friend from foe in the thick mist which rolled down, had slaughtered one another.

Both spellings together are to be found in imperial chrysobulls and other old documents, in Slavonic manuscripts. After the Serbs established themselves here they refer to the monastery by an abbreviated version of the same name, Chelandar or Chilandar.

The founders of the monastery were the Serbian ruler Stephen I Nemanya and his son Rastko. The latter, although a prince and heir apparent, preferred the monastic existence to the glamour of public life and the ceremonial of the court. Abandoning honours and titles, he came in disguise to the Mountain, where he became a monk with the name Savvas. He lived first in the monastery of the Thessalonian *(Palaiomonastiron)*. Later he moved to Vatopedi, where his father, who had abdicated the throne to become the monk Symeon at the Serbian monastery of Studeniča, eventually joined him.

Father and son remained at Vatopedi until the new Serbian King, Stephen II, requested Vatopedi to grant them the ruined settlement of Chelandari. This

35. Interior view of the monastery of Chelandari, showing the katholikon and the phiale as they are seen from the entrance.

gift was ratified soon after by the chrysobull of the Emperor Alexios III (1198) where it was laid down that it should be 'a gift in perpetuity to the Serbs'. Symeon and Savvas settled there and busied themselves with reconstructing and enlarging the buildings. They have thus, rightly, come to be regarded as the founders of the monastery. Stephen II, Savvas's brother, gave considerable financial assistance towards its enlargement.

Later, Savvas returned to Serbia where he became archbishop of the Serbs; Symeon stayed behind and died in the monastery. Both men were buried here, in the south-east corner of the church, and were canonised by the Serbian Church soon after their deaths. Urged first by Savvas, many Serbs began to come to Chelandari, with the result that the numbers of monks rose sharply. To accommodate them it became necessary to annex many smaller houses such as St Basil, the Komitissa, Kalyka, Paparnikion, the Omologitou, the Strovilaia and others.

Chelandari continued to enjoy prosperity for several centuries, and because of it the monastery acted as the main spiritual centre of the Serbian nation for a long time. Many of its monks acquired such a reputation for wisdom and learning that they were appointed as patriarchs, archbishops and bishops in the Serbian Church. Furthermore, at Chelandari many books were either written in or translated into Slavonic which spurred the progress and encouraged the intellectual development of the Serbian nation.

The monastery of Chelandari received many gifts and untold wealth from successive Serbian rulers. Perhaps the most generous of these was Stephen IV Dusan, who made liberal cash donations and conferred many privileges on Chelandari, as he did also on other monasteries on Mount Athos. One of his chrysobulls, which he signs as 'Tsar and Emperor of the Serbs and of the Greeks' shows that in 1347 he even visited the monastery together with his consort, Helen. The Byzantine Emperor Andronicos II Paleologos was a generous benefactor of the monastery too. Numerous chrysobulls bearing his signature are preserved here. One of these confirms Chelandari in its possession of the monastery of St Nicholas and other properties.

During the Turkish Occupation the monastery continued to prosper, thanks to assistance from the Tsars of Russia and the rulers of the lower Danube countries. Numerous Serbian monks continued to come to Athos, not only to Chelandari, but also to other monasteries. During this period a Serb was many times appointed *Protos*.

However, in the seventeenth century the decline of the monastery began, and accelerated after 1675, when the achbishopric of Pécs became dependent on the ecumenical patriarchate. The influx of Serbs slowly decreased. By the end of the eighteenth century the monastery was inhabited largely by Bulgarian monks. Amongst these was the great writer Paisios, who is famous for his *'History of the Bulgarian People'* and other notable works.

In the years 1722 and 1891, the monastery suffered two serious fires. Fortunately its valuable collections were left unharmed.

In 1896 the King of Serbia, Alexander I, visited Chelandari. He provided funds for its re-building and despatched Serbian monks there, so that once again the Serbs became predominant and regained administrative control of the monastery.

In the efforts made to incorporate Mount Athos into the Greek State both the *Protos*, who at this time was from Chelandari (1913), and the Serbian monks firmly supported the Greek cause. Similarly in the Second World War the Serbs were on the side of the Greeks against the occupying forces.

Like many other monasteries on Athos, Chelandari from the outside resembles a fortress, with its fortified enclosure wall and its two towers; that on the east side is attributed to the monastery's founder, St Savvas. A little way north of the monastery in the direction of the port stands a third tower, named after its builder, Miljutin.

The **katholikon** is dedicated to the Presentation of the Mother of God. It was built at the beginning of the fourteenth century and follows the Byzantine Athonite plan. The outer narthex is a later addition, built with monies provided by Prince Lazaros. The murals of the church were probably executed in 1319-20, a date suggested by several pieces of evidence. It is also concluded from the appearance of Miljutin amongst the portraits, where he is represented as an old man of about 70. This same king founded other churches in which his portrait also appears, each time at a different age. If his surmised age is taken to correspond approximately to the year in which each of the churches was built, we can arrive at an approximate chronology for the frescoes both here and elsewhere. Unfortunately these interesting frescoes were repainted in 1803-4. Nonetheless, we can distinguish some of their basic characteristics – their narrative quality, their mobile forms, their frequently unnatural stances and exaggerated gestures, the inclusion of local scenes and so on. In many of his representations the artist of Chelandari has surpassed the dramatic intensity, the impression of violent movement and the expressionism seen in the contemporary frescoes of the Protaton. These paintings are in the process of being cleaned, and several new scenes have been uncovered.

The magnificent marble *opus sectile* floor of the church is especially noteworthy, and so too is the post-Byzantine carved wooden iconostasis (1774). Behind the episcopal – abbatial – throne, in the *'gerontika'*, is the silver-covered tomb of St Symeon from which sprouts a vine whose grapes are a cure for sterility in barren women. Tombs of other builders of the monastery are also to be found within the church.

North of the *katholikon*, and approximately in the centre of the court, stands the **phiale** for the blessing of the waters. Covered by a cupola resting on eight columns, it was constructed in 1784 and painted in 1847, according to the inscription, by the monk Makarios from Galatista and his assistants.

The **refectory** of the monastery, a rectangular building with two apses and two entrances, forms part of its west wing and stands immediately opposite the west façade of the *katholikon*. It is decorated with frescoes by the Serbian monk and painter George Mitrophanovitch in 1623, which completely cover its walls. Striking Byzantine paintings of the fourteenth century, depicting Old Testament scenes, have recently been brought to light on the pediment above the northern apse.

In addition to the *katholikon* Chelandari has thirteen small chapels. Eleven of these are to by found within the monastery walls, and all except one are decorated with frescoes of periods ranging from the thirteenth to the eighteenth century. The two chapels beyond the precinct are those of St Tryphon, in the garden, and of the Annunciation, in the cemetery. In the latter, a few years ago, some interesting frescoes of the fourteenth century were discovered under the plaster, and others are still being uncovered.

Close to the monastery lie two of its *kellia*; one, dedicated to St Stephen, stands on the slopes of Samareia, the other, the Holy Trinity, lies in the direction of the Zographou monastery. Here, in addition to the frescoes of a later

36. Miljutin's tower, which stands on the rock between the monastery of Chelandari and its port.

building, the small apse of an older chapel preserves fragmentary paintings of the thirteenth century.

In Karyes the monastery has fifteen *kellia*. The finest of these is the old tower of St Savvas, known as the *Typikareion*, to which, according to tradition, the saint brought from Palestine the icon of the Mother of God still preserved there. Finally, it is worth mentioning the *kellion* of the *Molyvokklisia*, which lies half an hour north-west of Karyes. The church, dedicated to the Dormition of the Virgin, contains magnificent frescoes of the Cretan School, and a splendidly carved wooden iconostasis of the seventeenth century.

Only three of the former dependencies *(metochia)* of the monastery are still in its possession today, the Komitissa, about two hours from the monastery itself; *Zoodochos Pege* (the Life-giving Source) at the site of Kakavos near Ierissos and Kalamaria or St Nicholas at Sozopolis in Chalkidiki.

The monastery boasts a magnificent collection of treasures. Most of them are now housed in a modern building east of the *katholikon*. Far and away the most important is a collection of portable icons, many of which date from the Byzantine period and are preserved in perfect condition. The most splendid pieces are two icons of the Virgin *Hodegetria*, one made in mosaic; others represent Christ, the Four Evangelists, the Presentation of the Virgin, the Apostles Peter and Paul, St John the Baptist, the Archangels Michael and Gabriel, the Five Martyrs and many others. There are also five precious cameos; two are engraved with reliefs of Christ, two with the Virgin Mother and one with St Demetrios. There is also a famous diptych with twenty-four miniatures, the diptych of Ugliesa, a triptych dated to 1584, a Royal Door with a representation of the Annunciation, the work of the painter Mitrophanovitch (1616), a cup of the ruler Dusan, the pastoral staff of the bishop Synesios Zigovitch (1757) and many other objects.

In addition to the icons of the Virgin, *Tricherousa* (of the three hands), *Papadiki* and *Akathistos*, the *katholikon* houses other treasures. Amongst these are many embroidered vestments and materials, including two curtains, one the work of Euphemia (1399), the other of Anastasia (1556). There are also two crosses embodying fragments of the True Cross, a gift of the Emperor John III Vatatzis; another cross studded with precious stones; a splinter from the crown of thorns; the reed and the shroud of Our Lord's Passion; reliquaries containing relics of saints and many other items.

The manuscripts are housed in the same building as the treasury of the monastery. There are 181 Greek and 809 Slavonic codices, of which a total of 47 are written on parchment and the remainder on paper. There are 7 Greek and 5 Slavonic liturgical scrolls. The decoration of the illuminated manuscripts here is limited to headpieces and initial letters. The printed books belonging to Chelandari are stacked below the council-chamber. There are more than 400 documents. Of these 165 are Byzantine Greek chrysobulls; 160 are Serbian, 9 Russian, 2 Bulgarian and 31 Moldo-Wallachian documents, and 70 Turkish firmans and berats. The foundation charters of the monastery are preserved in this collection.

Chelandari from its foundation until the present day has occupied fourth place in the hierarchical order of Mount Athos. This place may previously have belonged to the monastery of Zygos, before it became a dependency of the Serbian house. Recently Chelandari took its place among the coenobitic monasteries of Mount Athos. The monastery and its dependencies house altogether some sixty Serbian monks.

THE MONASTERY OF DIONYSIOU

The monastery is built on a narrow and precipitous neck of rock, 80 metres above the sea. It lies on the south-west side of the peninsula between the monasteries of Gregoriou and St Paul. It is dedicated to St John the Baptist (feast day June 24th), and in old documents is referred to by several names, such as *'Nea Petra'*, 'the Monastery of the Great Comnenos' and the monastery 'of the lord Dionysios'.

The monastery was founded in the second half of the fourteenth century (1370-4) by Saint Dionysios of Korseos near Kastoria. He started this great work with his own limited means and, at first, with only his disciples to assist him. Seeing the magnitude of his task and the impossibility of its completion, Dionysios visited the Emperor of Trebizond Alexios III Comnenos and asked for his help. This was readily obtained because Theodosios, Metropolitan of Trebizond and brother of Dionysios, had interceded with the emperor on his brother's behalf. In the first instance Alexios gave a liberal donation, and followed this up with a yearly allowance so that the work should not come to a halt. Because of his particular interest in the new monastery Alexios asked that it should be called 'the monastery of the Great Comnenos'.

Later Byzantine emperors, especially members of the Paleologue dynasty, continued to help Dionysiou and gave it other grants of land and money. After the Fall of Constantinople in 1453 many Moldo-Wallachian rulers assisted the monastery. Their names are listed amongst its builders, for to them the monastery owes its enlargement and its present form. We should mention especially the names of Radoulos and of his heir, Neagoe Basarab. The latter gave money for many works including the tower and the aqueduct of the monastery (1520). The tower stands 25 metres high, and the last and newest floor bears a ceramic monogram of John the Baptist.

In 1535 most of the monastery was destroyed by fire. A short while later the ruler of Moldavia, John Peter, paid for the restoration of its eastern side, that is the section from the kitchen as far as the wine cellars. Later, another prince of Moldavia, Alexander, together with his wife Roxandra, rebuilt the six-storeyed wing whose many balconies overlook the sea. They also redeemed and returned to the monastery the properties it had mortgaged.

37. The monastery of Dionysiou, whose balconies, one above the other, overlook the sea.

Rulers were not the only benefactors of Dionysiou; other men of less exalted rank gave their assistance. These men incude the brothers Lazaros and Boios of Piavitsa in Chalkidiki, who rebuilt an extension onto the seven-floored wing; the brothers Thomas and Manuel of Serres, who built the buildings of the port and of the *metochion* at Orphanos at Mt Pangaion in eastern Macedonia; and finally, rather later, Makarios Bishop of Herakleia, Jeremiah Bishop of Belgrade (1797) and the Austrian Ambassador in Constantinople, John Frangopoulos (1800), all of whom took vows here towards the end of their lives and bequeathed their considerable fortunes to the monastery.

Many of the monastery's buildings which show little or no restoration date from the eighteenth century. That much building work took place at that time is evident from the wooden balconies of the individual cells, all of which look onto the sea, a kind of construction not previously undertaken.

The **katholikon** of the monastery, dedicated to St John the Baptist, stands roughly in the centre of the narrow courtyard. As the inscription above the entrance tells us, it was restored and frescoed between 1537-1547 at the expense of the Voivode Peter of Moldavia. The church, with its five lead-sheathed domes, is very dark inside because the surrounding buildings cut out the light. Its plan is that common to all the Athonite churches, with only a slight peculiarity at the eastern end where two apses, known as *typikaria*, flank the main apse as *prothesis* and *diakonikon*. Internally they are circular in plan, while on the exterior they are octagonal, covered by domes on high tympana.

The striking murals of the church were executed in 1546/7 by the painter Tzorzis, regarded as one of the most famous representatives of the Cretan School. He imitated Theophanes, but produced a different effect in the folds of the draperies and greater schematization and ascetic austerity characterise his figures. In the arrangement of themes, however, he follows the system of iconography found in the other churches. In the right-hand aisle are full-length portraits of the builder Peter and his children with an inscription. The narthex, which is linked to the western wall of the monastery, was decorated later by an unknown Romanian painter.

The church boasts a finely carved wooden iconostasis of the eighteenth century with exceptionally rich decoration; it is entirely cased in pure gold. In addition to some newer icons of 1805-1818 there are older icons hanging there, including five of the Great Deesis, the work of the Cretan painter Euphrosynos (1542). Elsewhere in the church hang icons of Christ and the Virgin, and a large cross, once part of an older iconostasis. In the sanctuary and the side apses, and elsewhere in the *katholikon,* are other icons of great historical and artistic value, dating from the fourteenth century onward. We should also note several reliefs carved in wood and ivory, such as those on the episcopal throne, the *proskynetarion*, the reading desks and the altar table which was fashioned in 1685.

Both within and without the precinct wall the monastery has many small chapels. The finest of these is the chapel dedicated to the Virgin of the *Akathistos,* to the left of the eso-narthex within the *katholikon*. Its frescoes, executed by the painter Makarios in 1615, were unfortunately retouched in 1890 by Michael of Caesareia, as the inscription above the entrance tells us. Within the chapel hangs an ancient icon of the Virgin made of wax and mastic, which is known as the Salutation of the Virgin. Tradition has it that this is the very icon that the Patriarch Sergios or some other bishop took in procession round the walls of Constantinople to give courage to the army and to the populace dur-

38. View of the monastery of Dionysiou seen from above.

ing the siege of the city by the Avars and the Slavs (626). The other chapels within the monastery are dedicated to St Niphon; St Nicholas; St George (1609); Sts Cosmas and Damian; the Archangels, with murals of the late sixteenth century painted by the monks Daniel and Mercurios; St John the Theologian (1608, with a narthex added in 1615) and St John Chrysostom (1782).

Outside the monastery in various *kathismata* and hermitages are the chapels of St Onouphrios; The Virgin; St James the Brother of God; St Demetrios; the Twelve Apostles and All Saints, with frescoes of 1610 by the monks Daniel and Mercurios.

Dionysiou owns seven *kellia* in Karyes; St Stephen's is the headquarters for the monastery's representative. It also owns a farm called Monoxylitis, a little beyond the *skete* of Thebais on the way from Ouranopolis to Daphne.

South-west of the *katholikon* the **refectory** has been built into one wing of the monastery. It was constructed by the Voivode Peter. Its frescoes, which show the strong influence of the Cretan School, especially in the paintings on the southern side, were executed in 1603 by the painters Daniel and Mercurios. Life-size pictures of saints and their martyrdoms, the Fall of Lucifer, the Assembly of Angels, the Heavenly Ladder, representations of Paradise and scenes from the miracles of Christ and the life of the Baptist cover the walls. Outside the refectory, in the cloister, there are other paintings preserved in good condition with many impressive scenes from the cycle of the Apocalypse. Finally, at the entrance to the refectory there is an old wooden door carved with various mythical beasts.

Close to the refectory stands the three-storey bell-tower, at the top of which is the monastery's old clock.

The almost non-existent courtyard is divided into three small corridors. Because space is so limited there is no **phiale** for the blessing of the waters, and other buildings or even trees, such as at other monasteries, are absent.

The domed **treasury** contains many valuable treasures collected over the centuries. The main items include an ivory plaque with a carving of the Crucifixion (10th century); the cross of Helena Paleologina, an *epitaphios* of the sixteenth century, gold-embroidered vestments and materials, much ecclesiastical plate, pectorals, crosses, patens for the consecrated bread, Gospels with rich bindings and many old documents such as chrysobulls, sigillia, dedicatory letters and letters bearing holy seals.

In a special crypt in the chancel of the *katholikon* the bones of St Niphon, Patriarch of Constantinople, are displayed. They are kept in a silver-plated reliquary in the shape of a church, the gift of the Voivode Neagoe in 1515. Finally, a case nearby displays many reliquaries containing some 150 relics, including fragments of the True Cross.

The **library** is richly stocked and well-organised. It is housed in a beautiful and secure room on the top floor of a new wing, recently constructed. It contains some 1100 manuscripts written on parchment, bombasine and paper, and 27 liturgical scrolls written on parchment. Most of these contain theological, ecclesiastical or liturgical works. A large number of them are illustrated with fascinating miniatures and richly illuminated headpieces and initial letters. Of special interest are codices 2, 13, 14, 61, 65, 587 and 588. Number 587 is an eleventh-century Gospel considered one of the best examples of its kind with some eighty miniatures preserved in excellent condition. Another manuscript, number 33, is an illuminated thirteenth-century Gospel Book which, in addition to its miniatures, has a rare wooden cover finely carved with many scenes.

39. View of the monastery and its port from the south-west.

In addition to the manuscripts the library contains upwards of 15,000 printed books, amongst which are valuable first editions and incunabula. There are also rare editions of the Holy Bible, of the classics, of ecclesiastical writers and various sixteenth-century dictionaries.

In the third *Typikon* of Mount Athos (1394) the monastery of Dionysiou held ninenteenth place amongst the twenty-five existing monasteries. However, since 1574 it has occupied fifth place. It is thus entitled to hold the office of *Protoepistatis* in the Holy Community every fifth year. Economic pressures forced it to adopt the idiorrhythmic way of life in the sixteenth century, which it abandoned only in 1616. It reverted again to idiorrhythmacy in the eighteenth century, but the coenobitic way of life was firmly established in 1805 and confirmed by the decree of the Patriarch Kallinikos V. At the present moment it numbers some fifty monks in the monastery and in its dependencies.

THE MONASTERY OF KOUTLOUMOUSIOU

This monastery lies close to Karyes on a sweeping slope thick with trees and bushes. It is dedicated to the Transfiguration of Our Lord (celebrated on August 6th). Other names for the monastery are 'the monastery of the Voivode', 'the *lavra* of the Romanian countries' and 'the monastery of Chariton'.

The most common name used today is Koutloumousiou. There is as yet no final and generally accepted explanation of its origin. Scholars disagree with each other, offering many conflicting opinions on the historical and philological interpretation of the word. Most follow the opinion of Uspensky, and argue that the monastery was founded by a Turk called Koutloumous. He is said to have lived at the end of the thirteenth century, and was baptised as a Christian with the name Constantine. Finally, we would mention here that in one document found in the monastery, which we recently examined, and which attempts to translate words with Turkish roots, the word *'koutloumous'* is interpreted as 'the saint who came from Ethiopia'.

Further light is shed on this theory by a document belonging to the monastery of St Panteleimon which is dated 1169. Amongst the signatories is the name of the monk Isaiah, *'kathigoumenos'* of the monastery of Koutloumousi. It is clear, therefore, that from the twelfth century a monastery bearing this name was in existence on Athos. It must be assumed that it is the present-day Koutloumousiou. Consequently, the hypothesis that Koutloumous was an Ethiopian only stands if we suppose that he was an Arab leader in the eleventh century, and that he founded the monastery either then, or a little later, but in any case before 1169. Other researchers, concerned with the general history of Mount Athos, advance arguments by analogy, and suggest a tenth rather than an eleventh-century date for the founding of Koutloumousiou.

In the twelfth century Koutloumousiou held the twentieth place in the monasterial hierarchy. The house was already in economic difficulties which continued until the early fourteenth century. The Catalan pirates attacked and pillaged it, causing its monks to flee and thus nearly bringing about its disappearance. To enable the monastery to survive at all, an Act of the *Protos* Isaac in 1334 granted to Koutloumousiou the ruinous foundations of Prophet Elijah and

40. Inside the monastery of Koutloumousiou, showing the phiale and part of the katholikon and refectory.

Stavronikita, as well as the old monasteries of Anapavsa and Philadelphou. Other Acts of the *Protos*, dated respectively 1312 and 1316, bear the signatures of the monks Malachias and Theodoros as abbots. In the latter document the signature is the seventeenth in the list, and may be taken to indicate the rank held by Koutloumousiou in the fourteenth century.

Koutloumousiou enjoyed considerable prosperity during the abbacy of Chariton of Imbros. Chariton displayed considerable interest in the monastery and made careful provision for its welfare, especially for the very necessary renovations and restorations. To that end he made several journeys to the principalities of the lower Danube, where he raised funds sufficient to rebuild almost the whole monastery, its precinct wall and its port. Of the many royal donors who contributed, perhaps the most liberal was John Vladislav of Hungro-Wallachia, who is consequently regarded as one of the monastery's founders. In his time, the second half of the fourteenth century, many of his subjects took vows at Koutloumousiou.

It was not easy, however, for these foreign monks to adapt to the Greek monastic way of life and to the austere rules of the coenobitic institution. For that reason, after the rebuilding of the monastery, Vladislav heeded the demands of his fellow countrymen and begged Chariton to change from the coenobitic to the idiorrhythmic way of life. This, of course, Chariton could not consent to do, but to make sure that John Vladislav did not withdraw his financial support he made the small concession of permitting the Romanians to follow the idiorrhythmic pattern of life, each according to his means. In return, Vladislav promised to provide for the building of the *katholikon* and the refectory, and for the maintenance and functioning of the monastery. At the same time the number of Wallachian monks increased significantly. Since they enjoyed the support of their ruler they attempted to impose their authority over the Greeks and even to drive the latter to leave the monastery.

Despite royal backing, however, their designs were thwarted by the firm stand and the persistent refusal of Chariton to give in. Chariton visited Vladislav and discussed the issue with him. The outcome of the effort was the written assurance of the prince that the Greeks should have precedence in the monastery, and that the abbots should always be elected only from the Greeks. The inter-relations of the two nationalities were finally resolved in the ruler's third will.

In 1372 Chariton was appointed Metropolitan of Hungro-Wallachia, although he continued to hold the post of abbot of Koutloumousiou. After his death, despite the agreement with Vladislav, he was succeeded by the Wallachian Melchisidek, later captured by the Turks. The crowning achievement of this brilliant period was the elevation of the monastery to patriarchal and stavropegiac status by decree of the Patriarch of Constantinople, Antony, in 1393.

In the early fifteenth century the monks of Koutloumousiou suddenly annexed the neighbouring monastery of Alypios, nearly deserted, on the pretext that their own buildings were insufficient for their numbers. To legalize their action, they sent a deputation to the Patriarch Joseph II who confirmed the union of the two houses in a decree of 1428. However, he imposed certain conditions which favoured the monastery of Alypios, for he himself had been a monk there. These conditions, however, remained theoretical rather than actual, and were never put into practice so that the monastery of Alypios eventually became dependent on Koutloumousiou. Today it is the *kellion* of the Holy Apostles.

41. Exterior of the katholikon of the monastery with the lead-covered domes.

The immediate result of this amalgamation was an increase in the prestige of Koutloumousiou. It became one of the finest monasteries on Athos, visited by kings and emperors, enriched by their offerings and gifts.

Nevertheless its prosperity was short-lived, and during the fifteenth century Koutloumousiou declined. The great fire of 1497 reduced it almost to ruins. To help its restoration the rulers of the Danube countries sent generous assistance of many kinds to Koutloumousiou or 'the *lavra* of the Romanian people' as it was called at that time. They presented it with many fertile estates within their realms; provided for the reconstruction of the damaged buildings and helped it so much economically that it is only right and proper that we should find their portraits amongst those of the founders. Of particular importance were Radu the Great, who sent large sums of money to the monks for the reconstruction of the monastery, and the Voivode Neagoe whose assistance made possible the completion of the restoration.

At an unknown date, however, the help from these rulers came to an end.

From then on Koutloumousiou was supported by Greek dignitaries, the pious and the devout. In 1767 a second devastating fire destroyed the whole eastern side of the monastery. On this occasion it was helped by the Patriarch of Alexandria, Matthew III. Formerly a monk here, he returned to Koutloumousiou after abdicating the patriarchal throne. The bequest of his personal fortune contributed towards the costs of reconstruction.

In 1856, by decree of the Patriarch of Constantinople Cyril VII, the monastery resumed the coenobitic way of life after many centuries as an idiorrhythmic house. In the same year, and again in 1870, fire destroyed a large section of the outer enclosure and many other buildings on the northern, western and southern sides. Fortunately the library, the *katholikon*, the sacerdotal vestments and the ecclesiastical plate escaped destruction. After these major disasters extensive repairs were carried out, made possible by the efforts of its capable abbot, Meletios of Lefkas.

The **katholikon**, which stands in the centre of the court, follows the plan of the other Athonite churches. It was built in 1540, in the time of the abbot Maximos. Of its five domes the central one is much bigger and higher than the others. The roof is lead-covered, and is much lower over the two narthexes than it is over the main church. Its wall-paintings, by artists of the Cretan School, were executed almost immediately after the erection of the church. Unfortunately they have since been painted over. The glazed outer narthex was built in 1744 at the expense of the hieromonach Isaiah.

The post-Byzantine, carved wooden iconostasis, with a series of horizontal panels and rich foliate decoration, was erected at the beginning of the nineteenth century. Various scenes are carved under the icons of Christ and the Virgin. Within the church at different points are some 150 portable icons, some of which are noteworthy.

A little to the west, opposite the façade of the church, stands the refectory, built with money given by the Patriarch of Alexandria Matthew III. Next to it is the **phiale** for the blessing of the waters (1813), and close by the free-standing bell-tower (1808).

In addition to the *katholikon* Koutloumousiou has many smaller chapels. The most magnificent of these is that of the Dread Protection (of the Virgin), to the left of the eso-narthex within the *katholikon*. It was built in 1733 by one Nicephoros and houses the miracle-working icon of the Virgin with the infant Christ on her left arm, his gaze cast upwards to the instruments of his Passion. Various prophets surround the central figures.

Other chapels within the monastery are those of St Natalia, in the guest quarters, which is frescoed; Saints Cosmas and Damian, All Saints, St Spyridon, St John the Baptist and the Archangels. Outside the precinct are three others; St Tryphon, St Nicholas and the Archangels. These chapels contain only portable icons.

Koutloumousiou owns eighteen kellia; that of the Baptist was the home of the renowned painter Dionysios of Fourna. It also owns three hermitages in the settlement at Kapsala.

The Greek idiorrhythmic **skete of St Panteleimon,** which lies close by, also belongs to Koutloumousiou. It consists of 23 *kalyvae* scattered throughout the woods; two of them are in ruins. It was founded by the monk Charalambos in 1785 on the site of the older *kellion* of St Panteleimon. The *kyriakon* was erected in 1790. A bell-tower stands in the court next to a tall, very old cypress tree. In the library there are some 40 manuscripts, written on paper, and 500 printed books.

42. The skete of St Panteleimon, with the kyriakon and some of the kalyves.

The **treasury** of the monastery contains some very interesting portable icons, sacerdotal vestments, ecclesiastical plate, crucifixes and many other items. In the sanctuary of the *katholikon* there are decorated reliquaries containing the relics of some 70 saints.

The **library** is housed in a secure room within the treasury. It contains some 662 manuscripts, of which 100 are written on parchment. There are many other old documents and approximately 3500 printed books. Some of the manuscripts are illuminated with elaborate decoration and fine miniatures (nos. 60, 61, 62, 29, 100, 412 etc.).

The monastery of Koutloumousiou holds sixth place in the Athonite hierarchy and, as we noted above, it has followed the coenobitic way of life since 1856. It now numbers some seventy monks living in the monastery and its dependencies.

THE MONASTERY OF PANTOKRATOR

Pantokrator is built on a headland lashed by the stormy waters of the north-east side of the peninsula. Its feast day is the Transfiguration of Our Lord (August 6th).

Two Byzantine nobles who lived in the middle of the fourteenth century are regarded as the founders of the monastery: Alexios the Stratopedarch and John the Primikerios. They had first lived as monks in a *kellion* called Pantokrator on this spot, which they gradually enlarged to form a monastery. Their efforts were assisted by John's relation, then Byzantine Emperor, John V Paleologos, who endowed the new foundation with a *metochion* on the island of Lemnos.

Later members of the Paleologue dynasty continued to assist the monastery. Manuel II together with the Patriarch Antony provided for the restoration of buildings destroyed by fire, and later John VIII made a generous donation. At the same time Pantokrator acquired rights over many smaller monasteries then in a state of decline; St Auxentius, St Demetrios, Christ the Saviour, Falakrou, Fakinou and Ravdouchou. Only the latter is still in existence, a *kellion* sited below Koutloumousiou. The rest are either forgotten altogether, or are mere place names.

After the Turkish Occupation Pantokrator experienced economic difficulties which Greeks or Greek-born rulers of the Danube tried to relieve. The most important of these was Blad III Kalogeros, who sent 1000 *aspra* as an annual allowance. Others include Neagoe Basarab, son-in-law of Helena Paleologue through her daughter Militsa, and John Mavrokordatos. Pantokrator, along with other monasteries, shared Russian benefactors; more particularly, in 1762 it received a donation from Catherine II together with permission to beg alms in Russia. All this assistance enabled the monastery to house about 200 monks, but it was not sufficient for the reconstruction of its buildings. Their renovation took place a century later.

The monastery has suffered from two disastrous fires, one in 1773, the other more recently in 1948. After the first, the treasurer Cyril worked tirelessly for the restoration of the buildings, while after the second the damage was repaired by the Restoration Service of the Greek Department of Antiquities.

43. General view of the monastery of Pantokrator and its port.

The plan of the buildings of the monastery forms an irregular polygon surrounded by a wall and a fortified tower on the west side. Most of the buildings are of recent date.

The relatively small **katholikon** lies at the northern end of the paved court. The co-founders, Alexios and John, are buried there. It is built in the style of the Athonite churches, with one slight irregularity. The distance between the choirs of the cantors and the sanctuary is greater than found elsewhere, and the *prothesis* and the *diakonikon* are housed in small domed towers. Furthermore, in 1847 the two existing narthexes were made into one, and a new glazed exo-narthex added. At the same period the archimandrite Meletios paid for the construction of the bell-tower which abuts the narthex.

The wall-paintings of the church date from the fourteenth century and are today preserved under a new layer, having been retouched by Matthew John of Naousa in 1854. Of the old paintings the Dormition of the Virgin, the Deesis and figures of various saints can still be distinguished.

There is no **phiale** for the blessing of the waters.

The **refectory** is built into a range of cells which face the west façade of the church. It was rebuilt in 1741 and frescoed eight years later by rather mediocre painters. The original refectory was below in the *'docheio'*, the store-rooms.

In addition to the *katholikon,* Pantokrator has eight small chapels within the precinct and another seven in its dependencies. Of these, the most noteworthy is the chapel of the Dormition of the Virgin left of the eso-narthex within the *katholikon*. Its frescoes of 1538 were painted over in 1868. The chapel of St Nicholas, close to the entrance of the monastery, and of St John the Baptist in the southern wing are also decorated with murals.

The settlement of Kapsala lies on the road between Pantokrator and Karyes. It consists of a large number of *kalyvae*, thirty-six of which belong to Pantokrator. There are also fifteen *kellia* scattered in and around Karyes. We would make special mention of the *kellion* dedicated to the Presentation of the Virgin called Ravdouchou, a former monastery which at the beginning of the fourteenth century occupied fourteenth place in the Athonite hierarchy. It must, therefore, have been in existence from at least the tenth century, the date of the painted representation of two crosses in the older *katholikon*, which forms a crypt to the newer. The paintings are found in an earlier layer, below those of the Apostles Peter and Paul which are dated to the twelfth century.

Another *kellion*, also dedicated to the Dormition of the Virgin, is called the *'Axion Esti'* (It is worthy). It is connected with the miracle-working icon of the Virgin now preserved in the church of the Protaton, but originally belonging here.

To Pantokrator belongs the Russian, coenobitic **skete** of the **Prophet Elijah** on a slope, about half an hour's walk from the monastery. Earlier a *kellion* stood there, which in 1757 was given to the eminent Ukranian monk and reformer Paisij Welitschowskij. The example of his life gradually inspired a number of Moldavians and Ukranians to become his disciples. As his followers increased, he transformed the *kellion* into a *skete* which followed the coenobitic way of life, the first example of such an institution on Mount Athos. The *skete* remained under Russian control, and the numbers of Russians dwelling there rose so high that they had to construct large buildings like those of the *skete* of St Andrew. This decision alarmed the patriarchate, the holy Community and the parent monastery alike, and the latter embarked on an endless series of legal wrangles to prevent the growth of the *skete*. These quarrels were finally resolved by decree of the Patriarch Neophytos VIII in 1892. The imposing new *kyriakon* was consecrated in 1900. It houses two noteworthy icons of Our Lady,

44. View of the monastery of Pantokrator from the sea.

the *Galaktotrophousa* (who suckles) and the *Dakrirrhoousa* (who weeps).

Of the treasures belonging to the monastery we would mention an *epitaphios*, a fragment of the shield of St Mercurios, sacerdotal vestments, ecclesiastical plate, richly embellished reliquaries containing the relics of saints and fragments of the True Cross, crucifixes, pectorals and many other items. There is a large collection of portable icons including several old examples of great artistic and historical interest: perhaps the most interesting is a double icon showing Our Lady with the Baptist on one side, and Christ and the Baptist on the other. Another icon of the Virgin, one of the finest on the Mountain, is to be found in the *katholikon*. Called the *Gerontissa* (the Elder), it portrays the Virgin standing, facing slightly to the left, in the posture of a suppliant. Athonite tradition tells the story that the icon once ordered a priest to hasten the end of the service so that the abbot of the monastery might receive communion before he died.

The **library** occupies a ground floor room in the newly built east wing. It contains 350 manuscripts, of which 68 are written on parchment, and two liturgical scrolls. Two manuscripts are illuminated; no. 61, a Psalter and no. 234, a Gospel Book, known as Kalyvitou. The printed books, more than 3500 volumes, are stored in the same place.

Pantokrator, which only recently became a coenobitic house (1992), has held seventh place in the Athonite hierarchy since 1574 (*Typikon* of Jeremiah II). It has about ninety monks.

45. Partial view of the inside of the monastery of Xeropotamou.

THE MONASTERY OF XEROPOTAMOU

Xeropotamou occupies a prominent ridge in the middle of the peninsula above the road from Daphne to Karyes. This beautiful and imposing monastery, dedicated to the Forty Martyrs (feast day March 9th), overlooks the calm blue waters of the Singitic Gulf.

Tradition ascribes the founding of the monastery to the Empress Pulcheria (450-457); other sources claim as founders Constantine VII Porphyrogennitos (913-959) and Romanus I Lecapenus (920-944). The former gave the monastery a richly embroidered red cloak. According to the testimony of reliable written sources, however, the monastery was founded at the end of the tenth century, that is to say a little later than the foundation of Great Lavra.

The probable founder of the monastery, the man who gave it his name, is the monk Paul Xeropotaminos. His surname is derived from the place where earlier he had lived as a hermit. He became the first abbot of the monastery, and was an eminent spiritual leader. His name appears in the first *Typikon* of Mount Athos (971/2). He was never a friend or follower of Athanasios, maintaining his own conceptions about the practise and rules of monastic asceticism. Paul, a stern ascetic and observer of the old ways, was the man who journeyed to Constantinople with other Athonites to denounce the innovations of Athanasios to the Emperor John Tzimisces.

At first this house was known as the 'monastery of the Forty Martyrs'. In other documents it was called the 'monastery of St Nicephoros of Xeropotaminos'. These may be two names for the same monastery; if not, we should perhaps assume that the Forty Martyrs belonged to a newly-founded and smaller monastery, under the protection of the older and bigger monastery of St Nicephoros. Yet another tradition has it that this was the site of the 'monastery of *Cheimarrou*' (the torrent), built by the Empress Pulcheria in the fifth century.

In the eleventh century the monastery of Xeropotamou was one of the richest foundations on Athos, since it owned large tracts of land on the south-west side of the peninsula. Its boundaries stretched as far north as the territories of Iveron and east to St Paul's, where today the monasteries of Simonopetra, Gregoriou and Dionysiou stand. With the passing of time its domains were inevitably curtailed, but even today its territorial possessions are extensive. The woodland surrounding the monastery is full of chestnut trees.

46. View of the monastery of Xeropotamou from the south-west. →

The prosperity of the monastery continued until the beginning of the thirteenth century. During the Latin Occupation it declined, and the monastery experienced difficult years when economic crises and the pirate incursions came together. After the regaining of Constantinople, the first Paleologue Emperor, Michael VIII (1259-1282), assisted the monastery financially, as we see from a chrysobull of 1275. It is said that he even visited Xeropotamou. His heir, Andronicos II (1282-1328) took care of its restoration after the fire of 1280, and secured its possessions by a chrysobull.

During the fourteenth and fifteenth centuries Serbian rulers, as well as the Byzantine emperors, gave large sums of money to the monastery. Their donations paid for the construction of the enclosure wall and the high tower, together with the small chapel of Our Lady on the north side. The *katholikon* was renovated in 1445.

Throughout the Turkish Occupation, and until the nineteenth century, the monastery of Xeropotamou passed through a series of crises brought by a variety of reasons. Firstly, its difficulties were due to the fierce raids of the Turks, secondly, to two catastrophic fires (1507 and 1609) and lastly, to the almost continuous legal disputes over boundaries with the adjoining monasteries.

Xeropotamou, though it suffered badly from Turkish assaults, lost more through the two fires which completely destroyed the buildings. Only the treasures were saved. Its subsequent restoration was largely undertaken by the monks, who collected large sums of money by travelling through the lower Danube principalities displaying the fragments of the True Cross. The rulers of these countries further agreed to make an annual provision for the monastery. Earlier, the Sultan Selim I (1512-1520) had distributed a subsidy and conferred many privileges on all the monasteries of Mount Athos, but especially on Xeropotamou.

The monastery received support also from many ecumenical patriarchs, particularly Timothy II, who by a decree of 1611 tried to ensure the continuance of the coenobitic way of life, and conferred on the abbot the right to wear a purple cloak. Later, in 1671, Methodios named the monastery stavropegiac.

In the second half of the eighteenth century, one of the monks, Kaisarios Dapontes, undertook the restoration of much of the monastery and built the portico, having raised the money during his eight-year tour (1757-1765) through the lower Danube countries to collect alms by displaying fragments of the True Cross and the relics of the Forty Martyrs. Dapontes imposed his will through force of personality, and was one of the most learned men of his age.

Catastrophes continued to afflict the progress of the renovation of the monastery, making necessary a succession of alms-collecting journeys. Only recently (1952) the Greek Archaeological Service restored parts damaged by fire and the reconstruction of the south-west wing, destroyed by fire in 1972, is expected to start soon.

Thus all the buildings of the present three-storeyed monastery have been built in the last three centuries.

The **katholikon**, dedicated to the Forty Martyrs, was restored between 1761-63 by Kaisarios Dapontes and decorated with frescoes about twenty years later in 1783. It stands in the centre of the paved court, orientated slightly to the north because of the slope of the ground. It follows the typical Athonite plan, although, except for the relatively small sanctuary, it is very spacious. Its walls are enriched by ceramic decoration. In one corner of the façade of the exo-narthex, a Middle Byzantine bas-relief with a full-length figure of St Demetrios has been built into the wall. The other bas-reliefs on the bell-tower show the heads of Pulcheria and St Paul, bearing the inscription 'St Paul Xeropotaminos son of the most reverend Michael, 1738'.

The carved wooden iconostasis, contemporary with, or perhaps slightly later than the church, is a superb piece of work. There are more than 200 portable icons in the sanctuary, the choirs and elsewhere: some of them are worthy of note.

Outside the church in the court stands the **phiale** for the blessing of the waters. Made of red marble, it was transported here and worked on, as the inscription tells us, by Kaisarios Dapontes. Its colonnade was constructed with the money of the hieromonach Seraphim in 1783. Inside the dome are scenes representing the Baptism and the Blessing of the Waters, while on one of the parapet slabs of the colonnade is an interesting relief depicting the monastery.

The **refectory**, built by the Wallachian abbot Alexander, is on the ground floor of the south wing of the monastery, opposite the entrance to the *katholikon*. It is spacious, and was decorated with wall paintings in 1859 by two artist-monks Sophronios and Nicephoros from the *skete* of St Anne.

Xeropotamou has several small chapels in addition to its *katholikon*, lying both in and beyond the precinct. The seven inside are: the Archangels, Saints Constantine and Helen, which are right and left of the eso-nathex in the *katholikon;* the Elevation of the Holy Cross; St John the Baptist; the Presentation of the Virgin; St Theodosios and St George on the four sides of the monastery. The three first are frescoed, the remainder contain only portable icons. Beyond the monastery to the east are its four *kellia*, the Ascension (formerly the Trans-figuration), the Birth of St John the Baptist, the Dormition of the Virgin and St Athanasios. At Karyes the *kellion* of St Demetrios serves as the headquarters for the monastery's representative there. The monastery also owns most of the buildings on the waterfront at Daphne.

The monastery has a magnificent collection of treasures. The most famous is perhaps the largest known fragment of the True Cross, which is contained within a wooden crucifix. In this fragment one of the holes left by the nails which fastened Christ to the Cross is visible. According to one tradition this was the gift of Pulcheria, according to another, the gift of the Emperor Romanos I. Other, smaller fragments of the Cross are displayed here along with the relics of many saints, many valuable episcopal staffs, two of which are made of amber, gold-embroidered vestments and liturgical plate, crucifixes, pectorals, chalices and many Gospel Books with rich bindings.

One of the greatest treasures of the monastery, which we shall describe fully in a later chapter, is the steatite paten 'of Pulcheria' of the type known as *panaghiaria*. A work of great skill and patience, it is just 15 cm in diameter.

On this relatively small surface are carved a host of microscopic figures surrounding the central scene, the *Hetoimasia* of the Throne.

The **library** is housed together with the treasury above the narthex of the *katholikon*. It contains 409 manuscripts, of which 20 are written on parchment and the remainder are modern and written on paper. A few are illuminated, mainly with ornamental headpieces and capital letters decorated with rich coiling tendrils. There are about 5000 printed books.

Xeropotamou today holds eighth place in the Athonite hierarchy. It was demoted to that rank in the early sixteenth century, having up till then occupied fifth place, now held by Dionysiou. It follows the coenobitic way of life and numbers some fifty monks, including those who live in its dependencies.

47. The port of the monastery of Zographou.

THE MONASTERY OF ZOGRAPHOU

The monastery of Zographou, dedicated to St George (feast day April 23rd), lies on the top of a rise, tucked into a woody fold, hidden from the sea. It is on the south-west side of the peninsula, nearly three hours' walk from Karyes, and an hour's uphill walk from its port.

According to tradition Zographou was founded in the tenth century, during the reign of the Emperor Leo VI the Wise, by three brothers, all monks, who came from Ohrid, the ancient capital of Bulgaria. It is said that the brothers, Moses, Aaron and John, could not agree to which saint the monastery should be dedicated, each pushing the claims of his favourite. One suggested the Virgin, the second St Nicholas and the third St George. Since none would give way to the others the decided to leave the issue to God's will. Depositing a panel of wood on the altar, they agreed to dedicate the church to whatever saint should find depicted there after several hours prayer. When they looked again at the panel they saw a representation of St George, and from this the monastery was dedicated to St George and called Zographou: of the Painter.

It is beyond doubt that the monastery existed in the tenth century, since the first *Typikon* (971/2) is signed by one George, abbot of Zographou. We know nothing of its history in the three centuries which follow because the records of this period have been destroyed by fire. By the thirteenth century it had taken its place in the Athonite hierarchy, and we know it to have been inhabited by Bulgarian monks, a fact which proves their presence on the Mountain from at least these years and perhaps much earlier.

Towards the end of the century the Emperor Michael VIII Paleologos conferred several favours on the monastery which makes one wonder how he, together with the Patriarch John Vekkos, both dedicated to achieving the Union of the Churches, should have tortured anti-Unionist Athonite monks. At Zographou in particular, twenty-six inflexible monks, believing in the Orthodox traditions and fanatically opposed to the Union, were burnt alive when soldiers of the emperor set fire to the monastery tower to which they had withdrawn for safety on October 10th, 1276. To commemorate this event an inscribed cenotaph was erected in 1873 in the courtyard, where it can still be seen.

A little later the monastery again experienced difficulties. The Catalan mercenaries pillaged and burnt it, largely destroying it. It was speedily rebuilt, how-

48. The monastery of Zographou seen from outside.

ever, through grants of the Paleologue Emperors, particularly of Andronicos II and John V, and with the assistance of many rulers of the lower Danube countries. During the same period several smaller monasteries were granted to Zographou; they include Our Lady at Xerokastro; the Holy Apostles, Kamilavkas and the Livadia. In the third *Typikon* of Mount Athos (1394) Zographou occupied tenth place in the monasterial hierarchy.

During the fourteenth century the monastery entered into a period of prosperity which, however, was not to continue for long. Gradually the situation deteriorated, and eventually Zographou was almost deserted. This time, the rulers of Hungro-Wallachia were forthcoming with assistance: of these, Stephen VI the Good was especially generous (1502).

The only eighteenth-century building at Zographou is the south-east wing (1716). Much is later. Between 1862 and 1896 the northern and western

49. Inside Zographou, showing the eastern range of cells.

ranges of cells, the refectory and the guest chambers were renovated, and the imposing portico constructed. The western wing, the highest section of the monastery, has very thick walls. In general the house experienced an increase in its fortunes in the eighteenth and nineteenth centuries, and it gradually came to be more wealthy than many of the other foundations on Athos.

At the beginning of the eighteenth century, and for a long time afterwards, Zographou was the home of many monks of Bulgarian and Serbian origin, as well as of Greek. This we know because the services were conducted in two languages, Greek and Bulgarian. But in 1845 Bulgarian supremacy was confirmed, and the house is still Bulgarian today. Its monks and other fellow countrymen who lived in *kellia* and *sketae* on Athos did not take part in the Bulgarian Schism at the end of the nineteenth century, and thus they have come to be known as the 'Bulgar Orthodox'.

In the second half of the eighteenth century the monk Paisios lived here and wrote his *'History of the Bulgarian People'* and other famous treatises.

The **katholikon** of Zographou is a recent building, erected in the early nineteenth century (1801) and frescoed in 1817. A stone in the south-west corner bears the date 1840, which suggests that this side and the glazed exo-narthex, were completed later. The church follows the usual Athonite triple-apsed plan. Its walls, of isodomic masonry, are built in alternate courses of dressed rectangular stone and bricks. Pieces of relief work, depicting various scenes, have been incorporated into the walls at different points in the four sides. The wooden iconostasis and the altar are finely carved.

The spacious **refectory**, devoid of wall-paintings, stands opposite the central door of the *katholikon*, built into the west side of the monastery.

The **phiale** for the blessing of the waters is preserved in very good condition near the north-west corner of the church. Built entirely of marble, its dome is supported on eight columns, and the interspaces of all but two are closed by parapet slabs. The water from the central fountain pours from lion-headed spouts supported by the marble figure of a monk. Unfortunately, the paintings inside the dome are very faded. In addition to the *katholikon* there are eight small chapels within the precinct, and another eight outside. One of these is that of the Virgin *Akathistos*, a free-standing building in the court next to the *katholikon,* with frescoes of 1780. Another is dedicated to the Thessalonican saints Cyril and Methodios, and is in the west of the monastery above the refectory. The others are the Transfiguration (1869), St John the Baptist (1768) and St Demetrios, all with frescoes; and three without frescoes, Saints Cosmas and Damian, the Archangels, and the Twenty-six Martyrs.

The chapels outside the monastery are all to be found within its dependencies, *kathismata* and *kellia*. Zographou also has two workshops in Karyes and one *kellion*, the Transfiguration, which is used as the headquarters for the monastery's representative there.

Of its treasures Zographou takes most pride in two large portable icons of St George which are displayed in the *katholikon* on the two *proskynetaria*. That to the right-hand side is said to be *acheiropoietos* (not modelled by hand) and to date from the time of the original founders of the monastery. Legend has it that a sceptical bishop, wishing to prove to his own satisfaction the truth of its miraculous fashioning, poked it with his finger. The finger was immediately cut off, and can be seen today stuck to the wood. The icon on the left-hand

50. Monument erected in the courtyard of Zographou to commemorate the monks burnt alive by the Unionists.

side, at least as valuable as the other, is covered with a heavy metal invest-ment made in 1882.

The monastery owns two notable icons of Our Lady, surnamed the *Akathistos* and *Epakouousa* (she who answers prayer). Both are the subject of leg-ends. Of the first it is said that an ageing monk was chanting unceasingly the *Akathistos* hymn in front of the icon when the Virgin warned him of the ap-proach of pirates. The monks had time to close the gate, and so remained un-harmed. The tradition about the second icon relates that the monk Cosmas im-plored the Virgin to tell him the best way to save his soul. One day he heard a voice instructing him to leave the monastery for a hermitage.

In addition to these miracle-working icons of Our Lady and St George, the monastery owns many relics, sacerdotal vestments, other portable icons, some of which are very interesting, valuable gold-embroidered cloths and *epi-taphioi,* as well as ecclesiastical plate.

The **library** contains 162 Greek and 388 Slavonic manuscripts of which 26 are on parchment. The remainder are written on paper and are of recent date. There are more than 8000 printed books, most of them written in Bulgarian.

At the moment Zographou ranks ninth in the monastic hierarchy of Mount Athos, and has followed the coenobitic way of life and administration since 1841. There are now only ten Bulgarian monks.

THE MONASTERY OF DOCHEIARIOU

Docheiariou lies on the south-west tip of the promontory, between the ports of the monasteries of Zographou and Kastamonitou. It is on the slope of a hill which descends sheer to the sea. It is dedicated to the Holy Archangels Michael and Gabriel (feast day November 8th).

Tradition says that the monastery was founded in the second half of the tenth century by Euthymios, supposedly a disciple of St Athanasios the Athonite. He was *'docheiares'* at Great Lavra, that is to say he was in charge of oil and other foodstuffs there. Originally Euthymios had founded a small settlement close to the harbour at Daphne, which was called Docheiariou from his office. However, a short time after its founding the house was dissolved, perhaps after suffering damage from pirate assaults to which its site too readily exposed it. The result was that its monks scattered; a few, still under the leadership of Euthymios, found a site somewhat removed from Daphne and founded the present monastery, which they also named Docheiariou.

An Act of 1092 gives us the name of the abbot then, Neophytos, formerly a patrician called Nicholas, who gave much assistance to the monastery. The same document tells us that from its foundation Docheiariou was dedicated to the Archangels Michael and Gabriel. On the other hand, Cyril of Docheiariou, in his *Proskynetarion* (or 'Worshippers Guide to Docheiariou') printed in 1843, notes that the monastery's original dedication was to St Nicholas, and was later changed to commemorate a miracle perfomed by the Archangels.

Slowly the monastery acquired its present form. As with every other monastery on Mount Athos, its history passed through many vicissitudes. In the tenth century, in the first *Typikon* of Mount Athos, it held the twentieth place and seems to have been enjoying a period of prosperity which lasted for some time. In the second *Typikon* (1046), it occupied tenth place amongst the 18 monasteries then in existence, and in the third *Typikon* (1394) ranked eleventh in the total of 25.

The fourteenth century was a time of financial strain, relieved by the help of the Byzantine Emperor John V Paleologos and the Serbian ruler Stephen IV. During this century Docheiariou acquired the monastery of Kalligraphou which,

51. Interior view of the monastery of Docheiariou showing its high defence tower in the background.

like so many others, no longer exists. Despite the frequent attempts to save the monastery, its decline continued into the sixteenth century since it suffered repeatedly from pirate attacks. Its fortunes only mended after the cure of the priest George of Adrianople in the waters of the well of the Archangels, which stands close to the *katholikon*. Sources tell us that he found the monastery virtually deserted, but as a thank-offering to the Archangels for his recovery he became a monk here and bequeathed his personal fortune to it for its needs (1560).

Seeing this example others offered help, including various rulers of Moldo-Wallachia. Most important of these were Alexander and his wife Roxandra (1568) who redeemed the estates confiscated by the Turks and returned them to the monastery. Yet other benefactors sent sums of money or presented lands, thereby supplying the means to help the monastery's recovery. It was at this time, the beginning of the seventeenth century, that the south side was rebuilt and the high defence tower renovated.

During the eighteenth century the bell-tower was erected, and the northeast side, as well as nearly all the monasterial buildings, were completed. The complex presents an irregular four-sided plan which takes account of the uneven sloping site.

During the years of the Greek War of Independence (1821-31) Docheiariou lost nearly all its treasures, as well as many of its monks.

The **katholikon**, dedicated to the Archangels Michael and Gabriel, stands in the lower part of the courtyard close to the west wing of the monastery which overlooks the sea. It is a high, spacious building, following the typical Athonite plan, with a very large eso-narthex. The present church was built during the sixteenth century thanks to the generosity of the Prince Alexander and his wife Roxandra. It was decorated at the time of its erection with paintings showing the vigorous characteristics of the art of the Cretan School. They are considered to be of a high stylistic and iconographic standard and are attributed to the Cretan painter Tzorzis (1568), who had earlier executed commissions at Dionysiou (1547) and in other churches on Athos.

The wooden iconostasis, richly carved with patterns and foliate decoration, was constructed by competent craftsmen in 1783; the canopy over the altar is an equally noteworthy piece of work.

Theophanes, bishop of Moldo-Wallachia, is buried on the left-hand side of the narthex. Having abdicated from his episcopal throne, he retired to Docheiariou and died as a simple monk.

In addition to the *katholikon*, Docheiariou possesses twelve small chapels inside its enclosure wall and three nearby outside. The most magnificent is the chapel of the Virgin *Gorgoepekoos* (the ready listener), opposite the entrance to the *katholikon* and to the right of the entrance to the refectory. Its name is derived from the miracle-working icon of the Virgin housed in the chapel, which is one of the monastery's finest acquisitions and one of the best-known and most respected icons on the Holy Mountain. Here two hieromonachs are appointed every year by the monastery, with the title of *prosmonarios*, to receive the numerous pilgrims and chant in turn their entreaties in front of the icon of Our Lady. They receive the oblations of the pilgrims, and are in charge of the maintenance of the chapel.

The other chapels within the monastery are those of the Forty Martyrs, the Dormition of the Virgin, the Annunciation, St George and the Archangels, Sts Cosmas and Damian, the Three Hierarchs, All Saints, Prophet Elijah, the Holy Trinity, Saint Demetrios and the Presentation of the Virgin. Those outside are dedicated to St Onouphrios, St Nicholas and the Transfiguration.

52. Exterior view of the monastery of Docheiariou.

In Karyes the monastery has the *kelli* of All Saints. The latter is used as the headquarters for the monastery's representative there.

The **refectory** is built into the western side of the monastery. It was erected through the generosity of Prochoros, Archbishop of Ohrid, and its frescoes were executed in the seventeenth and eighteenth centuries.

Apart from the icon of the Virgin *Gorgoepekoos*, Docheiariou owns a fragment of the True Cross, many saints' relics, ecclesiastical plate and vestments, a collection of gold-embroidered materials, wooden and wire crucifixes, chalices and other items.

The **library**, housed on the top floor of the high and imposing defence tower, contains 545 manuscripts, of which 62 are written on parchment. Some are illuminated. Perhaps the finest is a Menologion (no. 5) which contains many notable miniatures. There are also more than 40,000 printed books including many incunabula and first editions.

Docheiariou today occupies tenth place in the Athonite hierarchy and has forty monks. It has recently changed from being an idiorrhythmic to a coenobitic house.

THE MONASTERY OF KARAKALOU

This monastery, dedicated to the Apostles Peter and Paul (feast day June 29th), lies between the monasteries of Great Lavra and Iveron on a gentle slope high above the sea.

The many scholars who worked on the date of the founding and the naming of the monastery have reached different conclusions. Tradition has it that the first foundation was that of the Roman Emperor Caracalla (211-217), after whom it was named. John Comnenos, in his *Proskynetarion* (Pilgrim's book) accepted this view, while Gerasimos Smyrnakis modifies it somewhat, and suggests that the building work of the Roman Emperor may be only the port-tower of the monastery.

Equally lacking substantiation is the theory that the name is derived from the Turkish *'kara-koule'* which means the 'black tower'. The name Karakalou is known on Mount Athos long before the Turks first appeared to menace the Byzantine Empire. It is preferable to suggest that there may have lived a monk called Karakalas – a name common in various forms throughout the Byzantine Empire – who founded a small monastery at the beginning of the eleventh century to which he gave his name.

Karakalou is known to have been in existence by that date because it is mentioned in an Act of the *Protos* Nicephoros of 1018. The context is the definition of its boundaries with those of the Amalfian monastery. The fact that it is not mentioned in the second *Typikon* of Mount Athos (1046) may be because it was still small and of little importance, or it may be for some other reason unknown to us today. Nicodemos informs us in his *Pidalion* that he read a chrysobull of the Emperor Romanos IV Diogenes (1068-71) in which the emperor confirmed to the monastery an older donation of various properties. Unfortunately, the document has since perished and only the lead seal has survived. On one side it depicts Christ with Romanos and his wife, on the other the emperor's three sons. Another eleventh-century document issued by the *Protos* (1087) mentions Michael, abbot of the monastery of Karakalou.

From the eleventh century at least until the Fall of Constantinople (1453) Karakalou was not a prosperous foundation. During the thirteenth century it was virtually uninhabited, and was restored only slowly during the next century with the assistance of the Paleologue Emperors, especially Andronicos II

53. South-west view of the monastery of Karakalou showing the defence tower above the entrance.

and John V. The monastery also received help from the Patriarch Athanasios and the *Protos* Isaac. A document signed by Isaac records Karakalou's wretched state after the devastating pirate raids and the attacks of the Latin soldiers which alternately harried the monastery in the thirteenth century.

After this crisis Karakalou began to recover, and from official documents we learn that the number of monks gradually rose. Consequently its needs increased, and to meet them the monastery acquired properties in Thessalonica, Strymona, Lemnos and elsewhere, as well as the *kellion* of Exypolytos which was sited above the monastery.

Later, the house was again destroyed by pirate raids, and it was rebuilt in the sixteenth century by Peter, Prince of Wallachia. He redeemed from the Turks and returned to the monastery its confiscated properties (1570), and finally himself became a monk here. In the seventeenth century the King of Iberia (Georgia), Artchil, and his brother George Vachtag (1674), gave considerable help to Karakalou. About the same time the monastery acquired the dependency of St Nicholas in Ismailia. In the eighteenth century the house received assistance from the monk Joseph and many others on the Holy Mountain. The monastery then finally enjoyed a period of prosperity, and according to one document had at one period several hundred monks.

The quadrangular wall of the monastery surrounds buildings which are mostly post-Byzantine. Nevertheless, a few older buildings have been preserved, and thus most of the construction periods usually found on Athos are represented. We can distinguish three building periods: the first is in the mid-sixteenth century when the Sultan Suleiman acceded to the request of the rulers of Hungro-Wallachia and permitted the monks to renovate the monastery, on the condition that they did not extend its bounds or add to its buildings. At this period the *katholikon* was erected, the ranges of cells repaired and the port-tower constructed. In the second building period, at the beginning of the eighteenth century, many buildings were reconstructed and some additions made. The third period followed immediately after the disastrous fire of 1875, when the refectory, the south wing, the guest chambers and the northern section of the east side all had to be rebuilt.

Karakalou participated in the struggle to liberate Greece from the Turkish Occupation. It is well known that in 1854 the abbot Damaskenos presented the guerilla chieftain Tsamis Karatasos with a fine horse, an act which caused Damaskenos to lose his position and be expelled from the monastery.

In the second half of the last century many Russian monks took up residence at Karakalou in an attempt to gain control of the monastery. They infiltrated first the dependencies, scheming to convert them to coenobitic *sketae* and later to take over the monastery itself. They failed, however, to realise their designs.

An imposing tower tops the entrance on the south-west side. Preserved in good condition, it emphasises the fortress-like character of the monastery.

The **katholikon** follows the usual Athonite plan. It was begun in 1548 and completed in 1563. Minor repairs were carried out in the early eighteenth century (1707), and the bell-tower and exo-narthex added in 1710 and 1714 respectively. The frescoes of the nave were executed in 1716, of the eso-narthex in 1750 and of the exo-narthex in 1763. The subject of the latter is the cycle of the Apocalypse. A noteworthy icon of the Twelve Apostles hangs on the post-Byzantine carved wooden iconostasis. The icon is the work of the famous Athonite painter Dionysios of Fourna (1722).

The present day **refectory** was built in 1875 and is incorporated in the monastery's southern wing.

54. *Exterior view of the monastery of Karakalou.*

As happens at other monasteries where courtyard space is limited, there is no **phiale**.

In addition to the *katholikon*, there are seven other chapels, four of which have recent frescoes. There are four *kellia* at Karyes, of which one is used as the headquarters of the monastery's representative. Fourteen others are scattered in the woods north-west of the monastery, most of then now uninhabited.

Mention must be made, however briefly, of the monastery's port tower. It is the work of the prince John Peter and the abbot Germanos, and the inscription tells us that it was built in the first half of the sixteenth century, in the year 1534. It has a wall and crenellations, with the entrance above ground level reached by a ladder afterwards drawn up into the tower. Inside there is a small chapel and a refectory.

Amongst the treasures of Karakalou are a fragment of the True Cross, relics of many saints, sacerdotal vestments, ecclesiastical plate and other objects of historical and artistic merit. There are a large number of portable icons, of which we make special mention of the Kiss of Peter and Paul, the work of the painter Konstantinos Palaiokapas (1640), the Circumcision of Christ and others.

The **library** is housed in a special apartment east of the *katholikon*, and contains 279 manuscripts, of which 42 are written on parchment, as is the single liturgical scroll. The remainder of the manuscripts have illuminated headpieces and initial letters. The library also contains about 2500 printed books. In the archives are to be found several chrysobulls and other official documents referring to its history.

The monastery of Karakalou has followed the coenobitic way of life since 1813 when it was confirmed by a decree of Cyril VI. It occupies the eleventh place in the Athonite hierarchy, numbering some thirty monks.

THE MONASTERY OF PHILOTHEOU

The monastery of Philotheou lies half an hour's walk above Karakalou and some two and a half hour's from Karyes. It stands on a fertile plateau, traditionally the site of the Classical Asklepieion. It is dedicated to the Annunciation of the Virgin (feast day March 25th).

The first written record of Philotheou occurs in a memorandum of the *Protos* Nicephoros of 1015. Amongst the names mentioned is that of 'George monk and abbot of Philotheou'. In another document of nearly the same date (1021), Philotheou is referred to as the 'monastery of Pteris'. This document attempts to define the boundaries between the three neighbouring houses of Kravatou belonging to Great Lavra, Magoula and Pteris, that is to say, Philotheou. A little later, in the second *Typikon* of Mount Athos (1046) a certain Lucas signed in the twelfth place as 'abbot of the monastery of Our Lady or Philotheou'.

Other evidence, in addition to these documents, makes it certain that the monastery was founded in the last quarter of the tenth century. Such a view is not inconsistent with the legend which claims that the founder was a contemporary of Athanasios the Athonite, St Philotheos. This opinion is substantiated by a letter of accusation written in 1016 by George abbot of Philotheou on behalf of Paul Xeropotaminos.

The early history of the monastery is obscure. We know only that it received many bequests from the Emperor Nicephoros Botaniates (1078-1081) which made possible its construction. At the end of the thirteenth and in the fourteenth century the Paleologue emperors gave it considerable assistance, especially Andronicos II, Andronicos III, and John V. Furthermore, in the middle of the fourteenth century, in his endeavour to reinforce numbers in the monastery, Stephen Dusan published a chrysobull which had the effect of bringing first Serbs and then Bulgars to the monastery. That these monks, rather than Greeks, dominated the monastery for a long time is suggested by an Act of the *Protos* of 1483 where the abbot of Philotheou signed in Slavonic, not Greek letters.

In the early sixteenth century its abbot Dionysios rendered many services to the monastery and succeeded in turning it from an idiorrhythmic to a coenobitic house. However, because of the hostility of its Slavophile monks, who only left the monastery much later, Dionysios was forced to flee the Mountain. He settled at Olympos where he founded a monastery still known by his name.

At about the the same time, and certainly while the monastery was in financial straits, the Georgian ruler Leontios and his son Alexander provided the money for essential rebuilding. That the house was indeed in dire need is suggested also by the decision to sell the *kellion* of Stavronikita to Gregorios, bishop of Geromeri.

During the sixteenth century Philotheou and Great Lavra were engaged in

55. The entrance to the monastery of Philotheou, showing the contemporary decoration.

law suits over the possession of the *kellion* in the small seaside settlement of Mylopotamos. It was finally awarded to Great Lavra, but not without a complicated series of patriarchal decrees issued by Jeremias II and Mitrophanes, and Acts of the *Protos* and the Assembly.

About the middle of the seventeenth century (1641) the Tsar Michael gave permission to the monks of Philotheou to travel through his domains every seventh or eighth year, exhibiting relics and collecting alms. But this gesture was not sufficient to ameliorate the condition of Philotheou, which only improved in the eighteenth century when the Greek rulers of the lower Danube countries united to give their support. Thus in 1734 the chrysobull of the Wallachian ruler Gregorios Gikas set aside an annual provision of 6600 *aspra* on condition that once a year the right hand of St John Chrysostom should be sent to his principality for a blessing. A similar decision was made later by Konstantinos Mavrokordatos. This assistance, although available for only a few years, was sufficient to clear the monastery's debts and to repair many of its buildings.

The greatest personality in the monastery during the eighteenth century was the renowned Kosmas Aitolos, influential in both church and secular affairs, and chiefly known for his struggles to prevent the Mohammedanisation of Greece in the dark years of the Turkish Occupation.

In 1871 almost all the buildings except the *katholikon*, the refectory and the library were burnt. The piety of the monks sustained them in their affliction, and their hard work, together with the various donations, enabled them to erect the present buildings. Many Russian monks took the opportunity of settling in the monastery, their ultimate aim being its take-over, but their plans were thwarted by the determined opposition of the Greek monks.

The buildings of the monastery lie within a four-sided enclosure. As in other monasteries, three main building periods can be distinguished: the beginning of the sixteenth century, the mid-eighteenth century and the late nineteenth century. But building work at Philotheou has been more or less continuous, and even today its northern side is under reconstruction.

According to an inscription below the window in the wall of the right-hand apse, the **katholikon** was built in 1746, on the foundations of the older church which had collapsed. The frescoes were carried out over several years; those of the nave were completed in 1752, those of the two narthexes in 1765. The bell-tower was constructed in 1764, the marble floor of the nave laid in 1848 and the iconostasis painted in 1853.

The **refectory**, dating from the sixteenth century, forms part of the west wing of the monastery, immediately opposite the main entrance to the *katholikon*. It is decorated with some frescoes of the sixteenth century – possibly by masters of the Cretan School – no longer in very good condition. The **phiale** stands between the *katholikon* and the refectory and is constructed entirely of white marble.

In addition to its *katholikon,* Philotheou has six small chapels within its bounds. Two chapels with frescoes lie right and left of the eso-narthex, dedicated respectively to the Archangels (1752) and to St John the Baptist (1776). The latter has a very fine carved wooden iconostasis of 1786. In the bell-tower there is the chapel of St Marina; on the east side of the courtyard is the chapel of the Five Martyrs, and on the west are the two dedicated to St John Chrysostom and St Nicholas. Outside the monastery are three other chapels: All Saints in the cemetery, the Three Hierarchs or St Tryphon in the garden, and of the *Panayoudas*, or the Birth of the Virgin. Twelve *kellia* are situated close to the monastery, of which half are deserted. Another, dedicated to St Kosmas

56. The katholikon of the monastery with the phiale for the blessing of the waters.

Aitolos, is in Karyes and serves as the headquarters for the monastery's representative.

The **treasury** houses the relics of many saints, amongst them the right hand of St John Chrysostom given by the Emperor Andronicos II, and a fragment of the True Cross given by the Emperor Nicephoros III Botaniates. There are also crucifixes, many vestments and a collection of ecclesiastical plate. Easily the most valuable item, and that in which the monastery takes most pride, is the miracle-working icon of the Virgin kissing the Child, surnamed the *Glykophilousa*, the Sweetly-Kissing-One. Now covered by a silver-gilt investment, it stands against the left-hand *proskynetarion* in the *katholikon*. Tradition says that it is very old and that it was thrown into the sea at Constantinople by Victoria, wife of the patrician Symeon, to save it from the fury of the iconoclasts. It is one of the most revered icons on Mount Athos. Philotheou owns another famous icon of Our Lady, surnamed the *Gerontissa*, the Elder, said to have reached the monastery after a miraculous journey from Nigrita in Thrace.

The **library** has some 250 manuscripts of which 54, and two liturgical scrolls are written on parchment. We would mention specially a Gospel Book (no. 33), one of the oldest on the Mountain, with a miniature of the Evangelist Mark.

After a long period as an idiorrhythmic house, Philotheou became coenobitic on October 1st 1973, by decision of the Holy Community and the late Patriarch Demetrios. It has held twelfth place in the Athonite hierarchy since 1574, and now numbers more than ninety monks.

THE MONASTERY OF SIMONOPETRA

The seven-storeyed monastery of Simonopetra is the most daring building on the Holy Mountain and a marvel of monastic architecture. It rises from a sheer cliff high above the sea on the south-west side of the peninsula. It is dedicated to the Nativity of Christ (December 25th) in commemoration of its founder's vision.

This monastery was founded by Saint Simon who lived on Mount Athos about the middle of the thirteenth century. The story goes that Simon, who lived a hermit's life in this area, saw a light burning on the rocky ridge on Christmas night. He interpeted it as a command to build a monastery on that spot. Many monks, some of whom had been his disciples, offered their assistance, others their personal fortunes. Tradition further says that the first volunteers were so frightened by the dizzying heights that they decided to leave the site, abandoning the work in the middle.

Just as they were preparing to leave, Simon sent his servant Isaiah with drinks for the faint-hearted monks. On his way Isaiah slipped and fell tumbling over the projecting rocks. To the amazement of the horrified labourers, his fall was broken, and he stood upright quite unharmed. Not a drop had been spilt from the glasses he had been balancing on a tray. Thus according to the legend, the builders were encouraged by the miracle and carried the job to completion.

Simon called the monastery 'New Bethlehem'. It was only later that the foundation was named after its founder and the rock on which he had built.

The first buildings were made possible by the generous donations of the Serbian ruler Ugliesa in 1362. We learn from his chrysobull that he sent one of his overseers, Euthymios, with gifts and money to assist the completion of the monastery. Thanks also to other donors, the monastery began to prosper. In the third *Typikon* of the Holy Mountain (1394) it occupied the twenty-third place, and at the same period it owned several properties beyond the bounds of Mount Athos.

Later, however, a series of disasters curtailed this prosperity. A fire destroyed all the buildings, the treasures and the archives in 1581. The rebuilding was ravaged by a second fire in 1626. Thus, inevitably, the monastery was reduced to dire financial straits, and at the end of the seventeenth century it

57. The western range of Simonopetra. In the background are the ridges and the peak of Athos.

was forced to adopt the idiorrhythmic way of life. However, this did not achieve the hoped-for improvement of finances, and the monastery continued to decline. The situation deteriorated so far that at one point Simonopetra was virtually deserted. Fortunately, Paisij Welitschowskij along with other Serbian monks from Kapsala came to live there in 1762. Although Paisij himself stayed only a short time, he did much to help the monastery towards recovery. Later, Simonopetra received assistance from Joasaph of Mytilene, who collected money from various sources. He also presented the left hand of St Mary Magdalene, still amongst the monastery's treasures.

These successful attempts to extricate itself from its financial difficulties enabled the monastery to revert to the coenobitic way of life, re-instituted by a decree of the Patriarch Kallinikos in 1801.

During the years of the Greek War of Independence, Simonopetra, like other Athonite monasteries, was abandoned by most of its monks, and was closed for a short period.

At the end of the last century (May 28th, 1891) another terrible fire completely razed the monastery, including the *katholikon* and the library. The monks escaped only at the last minute and were able to save only the holy relics. Simonopetra was rebuilt with alms collected on visits to Russia, and the new seven-storey wing, on which building had already commenced in 1864 under the abbot Neophytos, was added.

The **katholikon**, dedicated to the Nativity of Christ, was reconstructed after this fire. It stands approximately in the centre of the narrow court, its narthex abutting the western range of cells. It is relatively small, and is as yet without murals.

There are many other small chapels belonging to the monastery. Within the precinct there are four dedicated to St George, St Mary Magdalene, St Charalambos, and the Archangels, all without frescoes. Beyond the enclosure are eleven others; in the cemetery, at the port, and at several of the dependencies, *kellia* and *kathismata*. Many of these were burnt in the great fire on Mount Athos in August 1990.

The monastery owns five *kellia* in the vicinity of Karyes. That dedicated to All Saints houses Simonopetra's representative at the Assembly. It also owns various other buildings, both in Karyes and in Daphne, which are rented to public services and private concerns. Finally, the monastery possesses the following *metochia* outside the Holy Mountain: the church of the Ascension in Athens; St Charalambos in Thessalonica; the church of the Annunciation at Ormylia in Chalkidiki; of St Artemios and St Antypas on Siphnos; and the church of Our Lady of Trygis on Lemnos.

Simonopetra, without being especially well endowed, nevertheless has some valuable treasures. Thus it owns a fragment of the True Cross, relics of various saints, such as the hand of St Mary Magdalene and relics of St Dionysios of Zakynthos, sacerdotal vestments, liturgical vessels, crucifixes, pectorals, valuable covers of Gospel Books and a few portable icons.

Many of the more valuable items in the **library** were destroyed by the fire of 1891. There are many fine illuminated manuscripts, which fortunately had been catalogued by Spiros Lampros. The monastery today possesses 123 modern manuscripts housed in its treasury. Compared with the other monasteries, its collection of printed books is considerable.

The monastery of Simonopetra is coenobitic, and ranks thirteenth in the Athonite hierarchy. At the moment it is prosperous and supports about sixty monks.

58. The several-storeyed south-east side of the monastery.

59. The New Skete; dependency of the monastery of St Paul.

THE MONASTERY OF ST PAUL

St Paul's lies beside a rushing torrent on the western tip of the cape, about twenty minute's walk above its port. Its neighbour, Dionysiou, is about one and a half hour's distant. The monastery today is dedicated to the Purification of the Virgin Mary (feast day February 2nd). Earlier dedications were to Christ the Saviour, Our Lady and St George.

One tradition claims a late eighth or early ninth-century date for the founding of the monastery. This arises from a confusion of two names; that of St Paul, who is supposed to have lived a hermit's life in the region of the present day monastery, and that of Paul Xeropotaminos, a contemporary of St Athanasios the Athonite. Another tradition holds that an older monastery on the site, dedicated to the Presentation of the Virgin, had been founded by a certain Stephen during the reign of Constantine the Great.

The most likely explanation is that in the second half of the tenth century, at the close of his life, Paul Xeropotaminos withdrew from the monastery he had founded and came to this region, which at that time belonged to Xeropotamou. Here he built a *kellion* between two torrents. The monastery founded in this same region was first called Xeropotamou, and only later adopted its founder's Christian name, a practice we have seen at other Athonite monasteries.

For almost two centuries following the foundation there is no reference to the monastery in documents concerning the history of the Holy Mountain, perhaps because it had been reduced to the status of a *kellion*. It is not until 1259 that it is mentioned in a chrysobull of the Emperor Michael VIII, which confirmed some properties to the monastery, then dedicated to Christ the Saviour. Following this, it seems that once again it was regarded as a *kellion* owned by Xeropotamou, reduced to this status perhaps as a result of pirate raids or the attacks of the Catalans.

In an Act of the *Protos* Isaac of 1316 the abbot of St Paul's signed in the thirty-ninth place. In 1370 it was ceded as a *kellion* to the Serbian monks Ger-

60. General view of the monastery of St Paul on the lower slopes of Mount Athos. →

asimos Radonias and Antonios Pegases. Thanks to their incessant efforts, it finally took its place in the Athonite hierarchy. In the third *Typikon* of Mount Athos (1394) the monastery of St Paul ranked eighteenth. In 1404 a decree of the Patriarch Matthew settled the boundary disputes between St Paul's and Dionysiou, and referred to the monastery as 'ancient'.

At the beginning of the fifteenth century the monastery had a number of benefactors. Amongst them were Nicholas, brother of Gerasimos Radonias; Radoslav Sabias (1405); John VII Paleologos as ruler of Salonica (1406); the Serbian prince Gkiour and his brother Lazaros (1416); John VIII Paleologos (1437); and the Serbian prince George Brankovič, who supported the first large-scale building programme at the monastery and built a new, more spacious *katholikon*, dedicated to St George.

Mara, daughter of Brankovič, wife of the Sultan Murat II and mother of Mohamet II, gave 1000 ducats and two estates, one in Serres, the other in Nea Roda, to the monastery. During the sacking and pillaging which attended the Fall of Constantinople, the Turks seized the fragments of the Gifts of the Magi preserved in a church there. They were later presented to Mara, who always adhered to the Christian faith. She wished to bring them in person to the monastery of St Paul along with other sacred objects. According to one tale, as she landed on Athos and prepared for the uphill climb, a voice from heaven forbad her to proceed further, explaining that here on Athos there is another queen, the Mother of God. Mara immediately halted and returned to the boats. A small chapel was later built on this spot to commemorate the event.

Subsequent benefactors of St Paul's are to be found amongst the rulers of the lower Danube kingdoms, both Greek and Romanian. They include Stephen the Great, Neagoe Basarab, who paid for the erection of the defence tower (1521), and Constantine Basarab who paid for the reconstruction and renovation of many buildings.

With the financial help of many rulers in the sixteenth century, the monastery entered a relatively prosperous period which continued into the seventeenth century when it supported some two hundred monks. Nevertheless, to meet its financial needs, especially to pay the heavy taxes imposed by the Turks and to repay the interest demanded by Jewish moneylenders, St Paul's was soon forced to sell many of its estates.

At the end of the eighteenth century its active treasurer, Gregorios, made journeys to many countries successfully collecting large sums of money which helped the monastery to recover somewhat. In the early nineteenth century his work was continued by another of its monks, Anthimos Comnenos of Silyvria, formerly an abbot in Romania and friend of the Patriarch Gregorios V. Comnenos took great interest in the renovation of the monastery, and gave it some properties on Kassandra and Thasos, as well as ecclesiastical plate and vestments.

The years of the Greek struggle for Independence saw St Paul's almost deserted. Many of its monks left, either to participate in the common struggle or to avoid the atrocities of the Turkish garrison on the Mountain. Afterwards, however, matters changed for the better, especially after the benefactions of the Tsars Alexander I and Nicholas I.

The monastery, built on a cramped site against a cliff face, could not expand in area and so gave its buildings height. St Paul's has suffered damage many times and for many different reasons. The two most recent occasions were the fire of 1902 and the floods of 1911 which together made almost complete reconstruction necessary. Its buildings belong to many different periods: the north side to the fifteenth century; the defence tower to the early sixteenth century; the renovation of the refectory to the early eighteenth century, while the nineteenth and twentieth centuries have seen the reconstruction of most of the remaining sections.

The **katholikon**, dedicated to the Purification of the Virgin, was begun in 1839 and completed on April 23rd, 1844, St George's day, according to the inscription on the external wall of the main apse. Its walls are of solid marble. The various parts of the church are divided off by columns which create a spacious effect. The present church lacks murals. A fragment of a painting with the head of St Athanasios the Athonite from the earlier church is preserved in the library.

In addition to the *katholikon* the monastery has twelve other small chapels. Two of these, St Paul's and St George's, lie right and left of the eso-narthex. The remainder are both inside and outside the precinct. Of these, the finest is a second chapel dedicated to St George, lying on the north side of the court, with paintings which are very interesting examples of Cretan art (1555).

The monastery owns three *kellia* in Karyes. That of St Andrew serves as the quarters of its representives in the Assembly. St Paul's also owns the farm at Monoxylites on the peninsula and some others beyond the bounds of Athos.

To St Paul's belong two **sketae**, the New *Skete* and St Demetrios.

The **New Skete**, dedicated to the Nativity of the Virgin (September 8th), is Greek and follows the idiorrhythmic pattern of life. It lies south-east of the monastery near the shore, and was earlier known as the *skete* of the Tower. It was organised and took the form of a *skete* about the middle of the eighteenth century. Amongst those who have lived there is St Nicodemos the Athonite. It consists of twenty-eight *kalyvae*, all picturesquely situated, and has at present about thirty-five monks. Its *kyriakon* houses 200 manuscripts as well as portable icons and ecclesiastical vestments.

The number of tombs and small finds, including coins, which have been found above the settlement, suggest that this site was previously occupied by one of the ancient cities of Athos.

The second *skete*, **St Demetrios** or **Lakkoskete**, lies on the north-east side of the peninsula between St Paul's and the tower at Morphonou (Amalfian). It was also founded in the eighteenth century, and is idiorrhythmic. Although it is made up of a *kyriakon* and twenty-five *kalyvae*, there are only a few Romanian monks living there.

In addition to the Gifts of the Magi referred to above, St Paul's has other treasures. We would mention especially a fragment of the True Cross, saints' relics, pectorals, crucifixes, ecclesiastical plate and vestments. A large wooden crucifix and a diptych are reckoned amongst the finest treasures of Mount Athos. There also portable icons, including the Virgin *Myrovlitissa* (flowing with myrrh), St George and the Deesis (a painting on glass) and many others.

The **library**, extremely well-organised, possesses 494 manuscripts, of which only a few are parchment, and about 12,500 printed books.

St Paul's has followed the coenobitic way of life since 1840 when it was re-established by decree of the Patriarch Gregorios VI. It ranks thirteenth in the Athonite hierarchy, and is inhabited by more than one hundred monks. Thirty-five live in the monastery, the others in the dependencies. Many Serbian monks used to live in the monastery, and for this reason its seal bears a double circular inscription in Greek and Slavic letters around an image of St George.

THE MONASTERY OF STAVRONIKITA

Stavronikita, dedicated to St Nicholas (December 6th), is built on a levelled headland above the sea, approximately in the centre of the north-east shore of the peninsula. It lies between the monasteries of Iveron and Pantokrator, about one and a half hour's walk from Karyes.

According to one view based on Athonite tradition, the present name of the monastery is the combination of the names of two monks Stavros and Nikitas. These two had dwelt in separate cells before uniting to found and build the monastery in the same region. Another tradition ascribes the founding of the house to an officer of the Emperor John Tzimisces, Nicephoros Stavronikitas, after whom it was named. Yet another opinion is that its founder was the patrician Nikitas whose name-day was September 15th, that is the day after the Elevation of the Holy Cross (September 14th), and that Stavronikitas is a compound of two words, *Stavros* (Cross) and *Nikitas* (the name of the founder).

Although the monastery is most commonly known as Stavronikita, and it is this name that has come down to us today, in old documents it is referred to as 'Of Our Lady', and more frequently, 'of Stravonikita'. This may have been its original name or a corruption of its present one. Some scholars believe that in the fourteenth century it was known as the 'monastery of Chariton', but this view is erroneous because we know that at this time the title belonged only to Koutloumousiou, in honour of its diligent abbot Chariton.

It is clear that the truth about the foundation of Stavronikita is lost in a mass of legends. Yet a document signed by the *Protos* Nicephoros of 1012 suggests that at that time an old monastery of that name was already in existence. In this and three other nearly contemporary documents a monk Nicephoros of Stravonikita is found as co-signatory. The same signature appears in the so-called letter of accusation of Paul Xeropotaminos (1016), this time as a monk of Stavronikita. In this form the name has come down to us today. This written evidence, as well as later documents, support our opinion that Stavronikita was amongst the many monasteries founded in the first wave of enthusiasm for the coenobitic way of life on Mount Athos.

It must be assumed that nothing unusual took place in the history of Stavronikita, and that its development followed the pattern of many other Athonite

61. View of the monastery of Stavronikita from the east.

houses, until the end of the twelfth or the very early thirteenth century. At this time it was almost deserted, the reason being, as so often, the frequency and severity of pirate attacks during the years of the Latin Occupation (1204-1261). The then deserted monastery was governed by the *Protos* for a short period, according to Athonite practice. Later, it was annexed successively by the monasteries of Koutloumousiou and Philotheou.

In 1533 Philotheou sold it as a *kathisma* to the abbot Gregorios of the monastery of Giromerios in Thesprotia, together with all its buildings and estates. This transaction was confirmed in 1536 by a decree of the Patriarch of Constantinople Jeremiah I, a friend of Gregorios. The decree also re-instated Stavronikita as a monastery, thereby bringing the total of monasteries on Athos to twenty.

Gregorios Giromereiatis, as he is usually called, soon left his own monastery and came to the Holy Mountain to begin the task of rehabilitating the ruinous buildings of Stavronikita. He enlarged it, building an enclosure wall and many cells and reconstructing the *katholikon*. As the numbers of monks increased he also pursued the annexation of the already ruinous settlement of Phakinos, then owned by the monastery of Pantokrator.

After the death of Gregorios in 1540, the labour of reconstruction was continued by the Patriarch Jeremiah. This was not only out of respect and affection for his friend, but also to satisfy the request of the Holy Community, which had an interest in the re-establishment of Stavronikita because of its exceptionally well-placed site. Jeremiah, sometimes from Constantinople, sometimes on his visits, helped to restore the monastery, spending large sums of money on its renovation and embellishment. After Gregorios, he is regarded as the monastery's second founder. He is responsible for the reconstruction of the whole monastery including the perimeter wall, the building of new cells, kitchen and infirmary, and the completion of the *katholikon* and its decoration. For reasons explained in his Will, he dedicated the church to St Nicholas, and he named the monastery patriarchal and stavropegiac. He succeeded in annexing the settlement of Phakinos despite the fierce opposition of the monks of Pantokrator, and endowed Stavronikita with many other properties on Kassandra, Lemnos and elsewhere, in addition to many estates both on and off the Mountain. He later bequeathed his very considerable fortune to the monastery to meet its needs as the numbers of monks increased.

Further details about the state of the monastery in these years and the progress of its reconstruction are to be found in two documents, Jeremiah's Will and Testament. From these two sources we learn that in spite of the adoption of the idiorrhythmic way of life, which at the time was becoming common in all Athonite monasteries, Stavronikita was founded as a coenobitic house and functioned quite efficiently as such for a long time.

However, a second period in its history opened when its fortunes began to decline, due to economic difficulties, small numbers and two disastrous fires.

One of the characteristics of this monastery has always been its limited resources compared with other foundations on Athos, and its very small number of monks. But even as the most recent foundation, however, it has received assistance in turn from the Holy Community, the 'archon' Servopoulos (1612), the hieromonach Markos (1614), the elders of the island of Kea (1628), Kourtessa, wife of Thomas Klados (1630), the Wallachian ruler Alexander Gikas (1727-1740) and many others. All these either presented land or made gifts in

62. The aqueduct of the monastery, with the defence tower in the background.

cash or kind to the monastery. Thus it survived these years, carrying out the necessary repairs to its dependencies and even buying some others.

But despite the number and generosity of its benefactors various factors combined to impede the development of Stavronikita. Most important perhaps were the continuous disputes over boundaries with neighbouring *kellia* and monasteries, especially Koutloumousiou. Stavronikita also suffered from various fires, for that great enemy of all the Athonite monasteries did not leave it untouched. One fire, in 1607, devastated the entire monastery, and only its records were saved; another, equally catastrophic, occurred in 1741. After both these fires the monks, together with outside help, worked to restore the monastery. The restoration of the *katholikon* began in 1628, followed by the construction of its famous acqueduct in 1680. In 1770 the refectory was enlarged, and three of the smaller chapels erected: of the Archangels, of St Demetrios, in the cemetery, and of the Five Martyrs, outside the monastery to the north-west.

During the Greek War of Independence Stavronikita suffered along with the rest of Mount Athos. Its financial position became desperate, partly because of its overwhelming debts, partly because of the contributions it made to the struggle for freedom. Its monks left the Mountain, either to avoid the Turkish garrison or to fight alongside their fellow-countrymen against the common enemy. Like many other Athonite monasteries, Stavronikita and its dependencies, both in the lower Danube principalities and elsewhere, were deserted.

Such was the state of affairs for a decade or so. As the Turks withdrew from the Mountain, those of the former monks who had survived returned to commence the task of re-establishing the monastic way of life. At this time the archimandrite Averkios came to Stavronikita from its Romanian dependency of the Holy Apostles, bringing with him various gifts and giving money to provide for the needs of the house.

Nevertheless, fresh calamities were in store for the monastery, which undid the work of previous generations. The successive fires of 1864, 1874 and 1879 wreaked considerable damage. Although rebuilding was carried out, the monks were once again forced into debts which later caused the house to decline and, once again, forced it under the guardianship of the Holy Community.

From this impasse the monastery was rescued by its industrious *proistamenos* Theophilos, formerly an archimandrite at Vatopedi. There was, however, no significant change for a long time, until the last years which coincided with the change-over to the coenobitic way of life. At one point the total disintegration of the monastery seemed likely from one day to the next.

Stavronikita is the smallest of the twenty Athonite monasteries. The tall crenellated tower which is particularly striking, seen from afar, surmounts the entrance as guardian and look-out.

The **katholikon**, dedicated to St Nicholas, stands on the east side of the very restricted court. It is the smallest of all the monastery churches, rebuilt about the middle of the sixteenth century on the site of the earlier church of the Mother of God, and restored in 1627-28. The narthex was added sometime after 1630. The church contains some fine murals in the Cretan tradition, executed by the famous painter Theophanes the Cretan and his son Symeon in 1546. The Patriarch Jeremiah I is depicted here as a founder, holding a model of the church. The inscription on the carved wooden iconostasis dates its erection to 1743 when the abbot was Gregorios of Chios.

In addition to the *katholikon* the monastery has several other small chapels

63. View of the monastery of Stavronikita from the south.

both within the precinct and outside in its dependencies. Stavronikita owns thirty-three of the *kalyvae* in the settlement of Kapsala, and four *kellia*, two of which are in Karyes.

The **refectory** is on the upper floor of the south wing and is decorated with very fine murals, probably of the Cretan School.

Of its treasures we should specially mention the very interesting mosaic icon of St Nicholas *Streidas*, (so named from the oyster clinging to the icon when fishermen dragged it up in their nets), housed in the main church. The splendid cycle of icons of the Twelve Feasts on the iconostasis dates to 1546, and there are also sacred relics, old sacerdotal vestments and liturgical and ecclesiastical plate.

The **library** is housed on the ground floor of a building north of the *katholikon* and possesses 171 manuscripts. Of these 58, and three liturgical scrolls, are written on parchment. A few are richly illuminated, (nos. 43, 50, 56 and others). There is also a large number of printed books.

Stavronikita was the first of the monasteries in recent years to change from the idiorrhythmic to the coenobitic way of life. All the others have subsequently followed its example. It has about fifty monks living in the monastery and its dependencies, and ranks fifteenth in the Athonite hierarchy.

THE MONASTERY OF XENOPHONTOS

The monastery of Xenophontos is built on a low hill close to the sea, between the monasteries of Docheiariou and St Panteleimon. It is dedicated to St George (feast day April 23rd).

According to tradition, the monstery was established in the tenth century, and named after its founder, Saint Xenophon. The saint is mentioned in the biography of St Athanasios the Athonite because he cured the brother of Saint Theodoros at Mylopotamos. Legend, however, identifies the saint with Xenophon, the Senator in the early sixth century who is credited with the building of the small chapel of St Demetrios within the original *katholikon*.

The first historical reference to the monastery occurs in the eleventh century, during the reign of the Emperor Nicephoros III Botaniates. An Act of the *Protos* of 1083 tells us that Stephen, Nicephoros's famous admiral, took vows at the monastery and adopted the name Symeon. He later became its abbot. Partly with his own fortune, partly with the help of the emperor, he took charge of the restoration and enlargement of the monastery. Both at this time and later Xenophontos acquired various properties on Mount Athos and beyond it. It seems likely that it was relatively prosperous at least until the Fall of Constantinople (1453) and the beginning of the Turkish Occupation. In the third *Typikon* of Mount Athos (1394), Xenophontos ranked eighth.

Its later history is similar to that of the other monasteries. It suffered repeated damage from pirate and other attacks. The repairs and renovations that these made necessary were carried out chiefly with the help of the Byzantine emperors and, after the sixteenth century, of the rulers of the lower Danube countries and other persons of rank, who in different ways provided assistance for the monastery and presented many gifts.

Xenophontos was the first monastery on Athos to revert to the coenobitic way of life after a period when, like so many other foundations, it was forced to adopt the idiorrhythmic one. The decision was ratified by a decree of the Patriarch Gabriel IV (1784), and was reached largely through the efforts of the hieromonach from Kavsokalyvia, and first abbot, Paisios of Mytilene. He also did

64. Exterior view of the monastery of Xenophontos.

much to restore and enlarge the monastery, greatly assisted by the very efficient treasurer, Konstantinos, and the archimandrite, Zacharias. Zacharias made journeys to several countries in his efforts to collect money.

At the beginning of the last century (1817), a large section of the monastery was ravaged by fire, which also destroyed the archives. Soon afterwards, restoration work began, directed by the former metropolitan of Samakovi, Philotheos, who retired to Xenophontos from his see. Concurrent with the rebuilding, the monastery was also enlarged. Philotheos did not live to see the completion of his work, which was carried out for him by the abbot Nicephoros from Kymi in Euboea.

At the beginning of this century Xenophontos supported about 130 monks, amongst whom was one of the most renowned clerics of the Greek Church, Nicephoros Kalogeras.

The new **katholikon** was built between 1809 and 1819 with money donated by Philotheou. It stands on the north side of the court and is impressively grandiose – the largest Greek *katholikon* on Mount Athos. It boasts a marble iconostasis made beautiful both by its design and the polychrome stone in which it is fashioned. Contemporary, and equally attractive, is the altar. There are no murals, apart from one or two recent examples in the *prothesis* and the eso-narthex, where there are two large and splendid mosaic icons, of St George and of St Demetrios. The icons of the Deesis and the Twelve Apostles in its right choir have probably survived from the iconostasis of an earlier chapel and are dated to the late sixteenth century.

The original *katholikon* still stands a few metres beyond the entrance to the monastery. Its narthex abuts the western range of cells and the refectory. Its very interesting frescoes are the work of the Cretan painter Antonios (1554). Other artists decorated the eso-narthex (1564) and the exo-narthex (1637). To the right of the sanctuary is a small chapel dedicated to St Demetrios, thought to be the oldest building in the monastery. Its carved wooden iconostasis is dated to the seventeenth century and is distinguished for its rich and delicate foliate decoration and the arched frames enclosing its icons. Apart from other evidence the age of this iconostasis is attested by the schematisation of its themes and bas-relief carvings.

In addition to the two *katholika*, nineteen chapels belong to the monastery, sited both within the precinct and outside in the dependencies. Eleven chapels lie inside the monastery, and of these four bear wall-paintings: St Euthymia, Saints Cosmas and Damian, the Dormition of the Virgin, and St John the Theologian. The others are undecorated: St Lazaros and St Demetrios within the original *katholikon*, St Stephen, the Presentation of the Virgin, the Holy Apostles, St Nektarios and the Holy Trinity and elsewhere in the monastery. Xenophontos has one *kellion* at Karyes, St Andrew, which serves as the headquarters for its representative there.

As we said above, a gallery connects the exo-narthex of the old *katholikon* to the **refectory**, where wall-paintings of the sixteenth century (1575) are preserved today under layers of later retouching.

Finally, we would briefly mention the **phiale** for the blessing of the waters next to the newer *katholikon*, the bell-tower (1814) and the two towers: of the Holy Apostles and of St Stephen.

Amongst the treasures of the monastery which deserve mention are two mosaic icons of which we have already spoken, a small icon of a kind rarely found, made of steatite and bearing a representation of the Transfiguration of Christ, a fragment of the True Cross, precious reliquaries containing the relics

65. View of the west side of Xenophontos from the sea.

of many saints, sacerdotal vestments, ecclesiastical plate and many other objects.

The well-organised **library** of the monastery is housed in a secure room on the south-west side. It contains about 600 manuscripts of which eight, and two liturgical scrolls, are written on parchment. It also possesses Turkish seals, various documents and more than 7000 printed books.

To Xenophontos belongs the **Skete of the Annunciation**. It lies about an hour's walk to the east, on a green mountainside with a fine view of the sea towards the Singitic Gulf. It is Greek and follows the idiorrhythmic way of life. Founded in 1760 by the hieromonachs Silvester, Ephraim and Agapios, it consists of a *kyriakon,* contemporary with the foundation, and twenty-two *kalyvae* of which few are currently inhabited. There are only seven or eight monks. Its library contains only printed books including some early editions.

Xenophontos still owns several estates beyond the Holy Mountain.

The monastery of Xenophontos ranks sixteenth in the Athonite hierarchy and follows the coenobitic way of life. Some sixty monks live in the monastery and its dependencies.

THE MONASTERY OF GREGORIOU

The monastery of Gregoriou, dedicated to St Nicholas (feast day December 6th), stands on a rock jutting out into the sea on the south-west side of the peninsula, between the monasteries of Simonopetra and Dionysiou.

On its present site Gregoriou was built in the fourteenth century, but it is not known what existed there formerly. Even the identity of its founder is uncertain, since two Gregories are often confused – Gregory of Sinai and Gregory of Syria. We believe that both should be regarded as founders; Gregory of Sinai because the first monks came from Sinai and Gregory of Syria because he gave the brotherhood the set of rules by which it lived and built the monastery in its present form.

More recent research, however, has suggested yet another possibility, namely that the founder of the monastery was Gregory of Sinai the Younger, disciple of the Gregory mentioned above. His relics are preserved in Serbia.

The first reference to the monastery in official documents is found in 1347 and 1348 when we learn the names of two abbots, Kallistratos and Kallistos. Later, in the third *Typikon* of Mount Athos (1394), Gregoriou occupied twenty-second place. About the same time another reference occurs in a report on the monastery of Zographou, which is signed by the abbot Averkios of Gregoriou. This document completes the very sporadic information available for the first two centuries of the history of Gregoriou, and the evidence remains scanty until the early sixteenth century.

Some part of its subsequent history is supplied by the famous Russian eighteenth-century traveller, Barsky. He saw several chrysobulls, since lost. It seems that Gregoriou was virtually abandoned in 1497, though the reason is not known, and that in 1500 the generosity of the Moldavian ruler, Stephen, provided for its reconstruction from the foundations. Barsky also states that the house was visited by the monk Spyridon, famed for his virtuous life. From a document of 1513 we learn that a large section of the monastery was destroyed by Saracen raids.

Barsky also describes another chrysobull which reveals that the princes of Moldavia continued to support the monastery until 1720. Other sources, however, suggest that assistance from rulers of the lower Danube realms continued until the early nineteenth century.

66. The port of the monastery of Gregoriou.

Barsky says that Gregoriou is the smallest of the monasteries, and that it consisted of three or four storeys in tower-like shape with a tiny domed *katholikon*, four smaller chapels, a refectory, store-rooms, kitchen, guest chambers, hospital and eighty cells. He describes its outstanding treasures and works of art, as well as a large number of documents which were later destroyed in the fire of 1761. The monks succeeded in saving only a few of the holy relics.

After the fire, the monastery was uninhabited for a time until its renowned treasurer, Ioachim the Acarnan, was in a position to rebuild it from its foundations with alms collected both from the Sultan and the rulers of the lower Danube principalities. Ioachim had been a monk at Gregoriou since 1740, but he had moved to the *skete* of St Anne to pursue a stricter, more ascetic life. He returned to Gregoriou only after the warm entreaties of many of its monks to undertake the work of restoration, This he completed in 1783, by his steadfast efforts and with the financial assistance of the rulers of Moldo-Wallachia, of Gregorios, Metropolitan of Hungro-Wallachia and many Phanariotes. Although he rebuilt the monastery on a small scale, Ioachim spared no pains to enrich and embellish it in every possible way.

Towards the end of the nineteenth century, during the abbacy of Symeon of Tripolis, the west wing was enlarged by the addition of guest chambers, several new cells (1892) and the marble porch (1896) outside the entrance. These and other buildings almost doubled the site occupied by Gregoriou, and it assumed its present form.

The **katholikon**, dedicated to St Nicholas, was first built by Ioachim, following the style of all the other Athonite churches. An inscription to the right of the entrance tells us that its wall-paintings were executed in 1779 by the painters Gabriel and Gregorios of Kastoria. In 1846, during the abbacy of Neophytos, the narthex was built and decorated. The wooden iconostasis is richly carved with scenes from the Old Testament.

Many treasures and portable icons are housed in the main church. The finest icons are those of St Nicholas and two of the Virgin, surnamed the *Galaktotrophousa* and the *Pantanassa*. The latter has survived all the fires and, according to the legend it bears, was presented to the monastery at the end of the fifteenth century by Mary Paleologina, mother of the prince Bogdanos.

In addition to the *katholikon* Gregoriou owns ten chapels lying both inside the precincts and beyond. They are: St Anastasia of Romaia (1775), St Gregory the Founder (1851), Our Lady and St Demetrios (eighteenth century), Saints Cosmas and Damian and St Spyridon (nineteenth century). Outside lie All Saints, in the cemetery, built in 1724 and decorated in 1739, St Modestos at the port (nineteenth century), St Tryphon and the Prophet Elijah (both more recent). It also owns three *kathismata*, the Virgin (eighteenth century) and the Holy Athonite Fathers (nineteenth century), close to the monastery, and St John the Theologian, high up in the forest.

At Karyes the monastery has four *kellia*, dedicated to the Purification of the Blessed Virgin Mary, Saints Cosmas and Damian, St Athanasios, and St Tryphon. The latter serves as the headquarters for the monastery's representative at the Assembly in Karyes.

The **refectory** is built into the south side of the monastery under the *katholikon*. It was constructed after the fire in the general rebuilding of the second half of the eighteenth century.

Especially worthy of mention amongst the many treasures of the monas-

67. South-west view of the monastery of Gregoriou.

tery are a fragment of the True Cross, the feet and right hand of St Anastasia and other holy relics, two gold-embroidered *epitaphioi*, old vestments and ecclesiastical plate, crucifixes, richly bound Gospel Books and many other sacred objects.

Many books were destroyed by the fire, and the **library** is relatively poor. It is, however, well-organised, housed in a vaulted room in the western wing. It contains 297 manuscripts, of which eleven are written on parchment, and some are illuminated. The library preserves the only extant manuscript (six leaves) of *'The Shepherd of Hermas'*, from which three pages were stolen and smuggled to Leipzig by the antiquities-thief Simonides. There are also about 6000 printed books including some valuable incunabula and old editions.

Many of its archives have been preserved, including patriarchal decrees, kerobulls and Turkish firmans. The oldest document is a Turkish *suret* of 1429 and a Turkish deed conveying property to the monastery in 1561 *(vakufname)*.

The monastery of Gregoriou has occupied the seventeenth place in the Athonite hierarchy since 1574, and has followed the coenobitic way of life since 1840. It now numbers some seventy monks.

THE MONASTERY OF ESPHIGMENOU

The monastery of Esphigmenou stands close to the sea on a peaceful inlet beyond the port of Chelandari. It holds its feast day at Ascensiontide (forty days after Easter).

Scholars differ widely about the origin of the name Esphigmenou. Some say that it is derived from the site of the monastery, which is hemmed in by the three hills of Zoodochos Pege, Samareia and Grimpovitsa. John Comnenos, in his *Proskynetarion* (Pilgrim's book) of the Holy Mountain (1701) says that 'it is called Esphigmenou because it lies bounded by three small hills and is wedged against the shore'. Others support the view that the name has some connection with the founder, or perhaps the restorer of the monastery, a monk whose habit was 'tied with a very tight cord'.

Athonite tradition attributes the establishment of Esphigmenou, like Xeropotamou, to the Emperor Theodosios II and his sister Pulcheria in the fifth century. But again, according to the same tradition, the original monastery was crushed under an avalanche which swept down the mountainside, and its ruins are to be seen about half a kilometre away. Both tales are probably to be discounted, and for the time being we know neither the founder's name nor the date of foundation. With some degree of certainty we may postulate a late tenth or early eleventh-century date for its establishment, since there are scattered references to it in documents of that period. It is mentioned in a letter of accusation of Paul Xeropotaminos dating to 1016, and later in the will of the monk Demetrios of Chalkeos (1030) where Theoktistos, monk and '*kathigoumenos*' of the monastery, is named as executor. Lastly, in the second *Typikon* of Mount Athos (1046), it is listed in fifth place.

Until the Turkish Occupation, the monastery enjoyed a period of prosperity. Byzantine emperors and the rulers of other Orthodox countries supported Esphigmenou, each in his own fashion. Especially liberal were John V Paleologos, the Serbian ruler Stephen IV and the Despot George Brankovič. Discordant notes were struck by the constant wrangling over boundaries and possessions with the neighbouring monastery of Vatopedi, by two fires in the fourteenth century, and by frequent pirate attacks made easy because of its sheltered site by the sea. Three manuscripts (nos. 4, 14, 286) preserved in the

68. The entrance to the monastery of Esphigmenou with the bell-tower.

monastery give accounts of such raids, which resulted in its almost complete desertion. The nearby monasteries of Chelandari and Zographou immediately seized the opportunity to appropriate some of its properties, thereby opening the way for new quarrels and legal disputes.

However, it seems that the monastery managed to overcome its difficulties. A document of 1569 tells of 51 monks working to restore the buildings. Later, after other misfortunes, Alexios the Tsar of Russia in 1655 gave his permission to monks of Esphigmenou to tour his domains every fifth year to collect alms. At the same time the Moldo-Wallachian rulers also made provision for the house, notably Gabriel Kostakis, who gave it the monastery of the Holy Apostles in his country. The number of monks began to increase at this time.

At the beginning of the eighteenth century two bishops took an interest in Esphigmenou. The first was Gregorios, Metropolitan of Melenikon, who came to the monastery as a monk and directed the efforts towards its restoration. The second was the Metropolitan of Thessalonica, Daniel, who put its finances in order so successfully that he was able to achieve its reversion to the coenobitic way of life. This decision was ratified by the Holy Community and the Patriarch of Constantinople Gerasimos. The final decree was signed by the Patriarch Gregorios V in 1797. He also paid for the restoration of the south wing, which had collapsed.

Many other works were undertaken at this time by a succession of capable abbots, Akakios, Euthymios, Theodoritos and Agathangelos, who are jointly responsible for the construction of all the present buildings. At the same period, a school of icon-painters functioned in the monastery under the direction of the abbot Loukas, successor of Agathangelos, who himself did much to help the monastery.

During the Greek War of Independence, Esphigmenou suffered greatly from the Turks because of its exposed position. Yet even this period saw some progress and development. In the middle of the nineteenth century many Romanian monks settled at Esphigmenou, only to leave again later.

The **katholikon**, dedicated to the Ascension of Our Lord, was built by the abbot Theodoros in the years 1806-1810. It stands on the site of the earlier *katholikon* and follows the typical Athonite plan. Its dedication service was conducted a year later by the Patriarch Gregorios V during a visit to the Holy Mountain. During its construction much assistance was given by the Metropolitan of Kassandra, Ignatios, who donated his entire personal fortune to the work. The large and imposing church has a lead-covered roof with eight domes, the central dome being the largest. All the marble for the church was brought from the island of Tinos, the home of its architect, Paul.

The nave was painted with frescoes in 1811 and the sanctuary in 1818 by the Galatsian painters Benjamin, Zacharias and Makarios. The frescoes of the narthex were executed in 1841 by the artists Joasaph, Nicephoros, Gerasimos and Anthimos. To the same period belong also the altar, the reading desks and the *proskynetaria*. The wooden iconostasis was carved in 1813 and gilded in 1846. Carved with rich foliate decoration and, on its lower panels, various scenes mainly from the Old and New Testaments, this iconostasis is considered one of the best post-Byzantine *templa* on the Holy Mountain.

The two side chapels, the exo-narthex and the portico in front of the entrance to the church were all added in 1845 by the Patriarch Anthimos VI, a monk at Esphigmenou before his promotion.

Outside the south-east corner of the *katholikon* stands the **phiale** for the blessing of the waters. It was erected in 1815 by the abbot Euthymios on the

69. The katholikon and part of the courtyard of the monastery.

site of the original *phiale* which dated from the time of the Emperor John V Paleologos. Its dome is supported on eight columns and closed in at the base by marble parapet slabs bearing relief decoration.

The **refectory** stands opposite the western façade of the *katholikon*. It too was restored by Euthymios, and is a rectangular free-standing building in the court (1810), capable of seating about one hundred persons. Its frescoes (1811) have been much blackened by the smoke from fires lit by the Turkish garrison which occupied the monastery during the Greek War of Independence.

Thirteen smaller chapels belong to the monastery in addition to its *katholikon*, eight within the precincts and five outside. Of those inside the monastery the two finest are the Presentation of the Virgin and the Archangels, right and

left of the eso-narthex of the *katholikon*. The other six are sited in the various ranges of buildings and include Saints Cosmas and Damian in the hospital, St Anthimos, next to the abbot's quarters, in which the tonsuring of novices takes place, St George, in the south-east corner, with a fine carved wooden iconostasis, Saints Constantine and Helen above the entrance to the monastery (1854) and Saints Gregorios Palamas, Neilos the Wise, Neilos the Myrovletes and John the Merciful in the east wing. None of these has frescoes, although they all contain portable icons, in some of which the hand of the painter Loukas, or Papa-Loukas, can be discerned.

Of the chapels which lie outside the precincts one in particular should be mentioned, that of St Antony Pechersky. It is sited opposite the monastery. St Antony established the Lavra at Kiev and is also considered as the founder of monasticism in Russia on the model of Greek monastic institutions familiar to him. The remaining chapels are the Dormition of the Virgin, in the cemetery, St Modestos, Saints Theodore and All Saints.

Esphigmenou owns one *kellion* and a three-storeyed building in Karyes.

Many of the monastery's treasures are housed in the **treasury** which, for the time being, is under the same roof as the manuscript library above the narthex of the *katholikon*. Here are kept crucifixes, pectorals, sacerdotal vestments, ecclesiastical plate and many other items. Esphigmenou also owns a large piece (3.05 x 2.80 m.) of the tent of the Emperor Napoleon. Presented by

70. General view of the monastery from the sea.

the Patriarch Gregory V, it serves once a year, on the occasion of the feast day of the monastery at Ascensiontide, as the curtain to the central entrance to the main church.

Other treasures are displayed in the sanctuary. Here may be seen the so-called cross of Pulcheria, reliquaries, many relics of saints, and a very fine Byzantine mosaic icon, measuring only 0.15 x 0.07 m. It depicts a full-length frontal image of Christ, his right hand raised in blessing, his left holding a closed gospel book. It is surrounded by a silver frame carrying depictions of the Apostles, while the bottom part is studded with holy relics. Finally, in the original abbot's quarters, are the portable icons and the archives containing chrysobulls, lead-sealed bulls, patriarchal decrees and other documents.

The **library**, also in the space above the narthex, is reached by a spiral staircase. It contains 372 manuscripts of which 75 are written on parchment and a few illuminated. The finest is an eleventh-century Menologion (no. 14) which contains 80 miniatures. There are also about 2000 printed books here and another 7000 kept on the second floor of the north wing.

The monastery of Esphigmenou follows the coenobitic way of life, and now occupies the eighteenth place in the Athonite hierarchy. It supports some sixty-five monks.

131

71. *Interior view of the monastery of St Panteleimon showing the katholikon with its many distinctive onion-shaped domes.*

THE MONASTERY OF ST PANTELEIMON

The monastery of St Panteleimon is built on an inlet of the Singitic Gulf beyond Xenophontos and before reaching Daphne. Dedicated to St Panteleimon
(feast day July 27th), it is also known as *'ton Rosson'* (of the Russians), 'the
coenobium of the Kallimachides' or simply 'Roussikon'.

The monastery was laid out on its present site above the sea after 1765,
perhaps as late as the first decades of the last century. It was originally founded on the site now known as Palaiomonastiron, that is to say, the old monastery of St Panteleimon or the monastery of the Thessalonian, founded at the
beginning of the eleventh century. At that time monks from Russia and Dalma-
tia arrived on Mount Athos and settled at the monastery of Xylourgos. Their
numbers slowly increased, and, at the instigation of the abbot Laurentios and
the *Protos*, the Holy Community granted them the then deserted monastery of
the Thessalonian. Xylourgos later sank to the status of *skete* (Bogoroditsa),
which it still is today.

No sources exist to detail the fortunes of the monastery before the thirteenth century, possibly because at that time both the buildings and the archives were destroyed by fire. The earliest record is a chrysobull of Andronicos II Paleologos which confirmed all the properties and privileges of the monastery. Later, many Serbian rulers made provision for the house, presenting it
with *metochia* and endowing it with treasures.

Despite the title 'the monastery of the Russians', the abbot of the monastery at this time always signed documents in Greek. This suggests that more
Greek than Russian monks lived there, a situation which lasted until 1497, the
year in which the Russians were freed from the Mongol yoke. Immediately
many more Russians came to St Panteleimon, soon outnumbering the Greeks.

In the third *Typikon* of Mount Athos (1394) the monastery occupied fifth
place in the Athonite hierarchy. But after a brief period of prosperity, St Panteleimon again declined and slipped into such poverty that it was forced to bor-
row large sums of money, using its ecclesiastical plate, the holy vestments
and many of its properties as security. This state of affairs continued into the
middle of the eighteenth century, and, finally, it was quite literally forced to
shut its gates. Thus the traveller Barsky tells us that on his first visit he found

72. Exterior view of the monastery and the several-storeyed buildings near the sea. →

only four monks, two Russian and two Bulgarian, but on his second visit the monastery was totally deserted. The house thus passed under Greek control and its Greek inhabitants decided to abandon the old buildings and move closer to the sea, to a site where the Bishop of Ierissos, Christophoros, had erected the small church of the Resurrection (1667). At this spot the new monastery of St Panteleimon was established, greatly assisted by the beneficence and goodwill of the rulers of the lower Danube countries and by the sale of its properties there.

The construction of the present monastery was carried out in the first two decades of the last century, largely with the help of the ruler of Moldo-Wallachia, Skarlatos Kallimaches, who also built the *katholikon*. The Patriarch Kallinikos V confirmed the coenobitic way of life there in 1803, and decreed that the monastery should enjoy the title of 'the true Coenobium of the Kallimachides'.

The outbreak of the War of Independence once more precipitated an economic crisis at St Panteleimon. After its conclusion the monastery was engaged in lawsuits over boundaries with the neighbouring monastery of Xenophontos. Although it was in a state of wretched poverty, by 1840 it began again to admit Russians as monks, whose numbers increased so rapidly that they soon constituted the majority. A new period in the monastery's history opened and, as was to be expected, one of their number was elected as abbot (1875). Thus the monastery passed entirely under Russian control. At the end of the nineteenth century St Panteleimon supported more than one thousand Russian monks, while many other Russians lived elsewhere on the Holy Mountain.

The monastery consists of so vast a complex of buildings of different heights, dominated by the high domes of its many churches, that it gives the impression of a small township. Until the most recent fire (1968) one wing of the monastery, including a large hall decorated with photographs of the Tsars, was used as the guest quarters. Since 1968 some of the large buildings close to the sea, no longer serving any of the miscellaneous purposes for which they were erected, have been turned into guest chambers.

An inscription above the entrance to the eso-narthex informs us that the **katholikon** was begun in 1812 and completed in 1821. It is dedicated to St Panteleimon and is built in the style of all the Athonite churches. Its walls are constructed of dressed stone and support eight domes, which unlike any others on Mount Athos, resemble the onion-domes of eastern Europe and terminate in a gilded cross. Similar shaped domes roof the smaller chapels of the monastery. The interior of the *katholikon* is covered with frescoes in the Russian style, dating from the last century. Similarly, the richly decorated iconostasis is of Russian inspiration. A decree of 1875 laid down that the services held in the church must be chanted in both Greek and Russian, and this practice is still observed.

The **refectory**, a free-standing rectangular building, stands opposite the entrance to the *katholikon*. It was erected in 1890 and its frescoes executed in 1897. It is extremely large, having been planned to seat about 800 people.

Above the entrance to the refectory rises a belfry in which hangs a set of Russian bells of different sizes. Immediately in front of the refectory, left of the entrance, stands the uniquely designed **phiale**. It bears no resemblance to any other found on Mount Athos.

In addition to the *katholikon* there are many other small chapels both inside and outside the monastery. Within the quadrangle is the chapel dedicated to the Dormition of the Virgin, immediately behind the *katholikon*, and that of St Metrophanes west of the library. In the former the services are conducted in Greek, in the latter in Russian. The northern wing of the monastery contains nine chapels: those of the Ascension, St Sergios, St Demetrios, the Archangels, St Gerasimos, Saints Constantine and Helen, Vladimir and Olga, the saints and isapostles of Russia, the twin chapels of St Alexander Nevskij and the Holy Canopy. This chapel is richly decorated inside with many gold-invested icons and a gilded iconostasis. Only two chapels on the southern side of the monastery, St Savvas and St Nicholas, survived the fire of 1968, which destroyed six others.

Beyond the monastery are two other chapels: one, in the cemetery, is dedicated to the Saints Peter, Alexios, Jonas and Philip – all metropolitan bishops of Moscow; the other, in the present day guest quarters, to the Transfiguration. St Panteleimon also owns five *kellia*, those of St Euthymios, Saints Cosmas and Damian, Zoodochos Pege and, in Karyes, St Stephen and St George. The latter serves as the headquarters for the monastery's representative there.

To St Panteleimon belong four dependencies; the *metochion* of Chromitsa or Chromitissa at the northern end of the peninsula close to Ouranopolis, where only a few Russian monks now remain to follow the coenobitic way of life: the *skete* of Xylourgou or Bogoroditsa (of Our Lady) which is also coenobitic and inhabited by a few Bulgarian monks, built in the region of the monastery of Pantokrator: Nea Thebais or Gournoskete, the most southwesterly settlement on Athos, and Palaiomonastiron, both now abandoned.

The treasures of the monastery include numerous portable icons, such as Our Lady of Jerusalem, St John the Baptist, St Panteleimon and a mosaic icon of St Alexander Nevskij. There are also many sacerdotal vestments, mainly of Russian manufacture, crucifixes, pectorals, fragments of the True Cross and holy relics. In the chapel of the Holy Canopy is a very fine chalice and a valuable printed copy of the Gospels, both gifts of Grand Duke Constantine Nicholayevič who visited the monastery in 1845.

The **library**, housed in a two-storeyed building in the court, is rich in books and manuscripts. It contains some 1320 Greek and another 600 Slavonic manuscripts, as well as leaves of parchment or paper codices now in folders. Of the many illuminated manuscripts we would mention two of the most richly illustrated, no. 2, a Gospel Lectionary and no. 6, the Sixteen Homilies of St Gregory the Theologian. The library also contains more than 20,000 printed books in both Greek and Russian, amongst which are some rare editions.

The monastery of St Panteleimon has followed the coenobitic way of life since 1803 and now holds nineteenth place in the Athonite hierarchy. It supports about thirty monks, of whom only one is Greek.

THE MONASTERY OF KASTAMONITOU

Kastamonitou is one of the most picturesquely sited monasteries on the Holy Mountain, hidden from the sea in the depths of a green forest above the Singitic Gulf. It is about half an hour's walk from the sea, from which point only its port is visible. On one side lies the monastery of Zographou, on the other Docheiariou. It is dedicated to the first martyr, St Stephen (feast day December 27th).

Both the date of the founding and the origin of the name are surrounded by legend. One tradition ascribes the foundation to the Emperor Constantine the Great in the fourth century or to his son Constans, after whom it should supposedly be named, Konstamonitou. According to another tradition, the monastery was established by an ascetic born at Kastamoni in Asia Minor, and to yet another tale by an ascetic called Kastamonitis, a name commonly found in Byzantine documents especially at the period when this monastery is most likely to have been founded. The opinion of some scholars that the name is derived from the number of chestnut trees *'kastanies'* which surround the monastery seems improbable.

Although the monastery is mentioned in various documents as early as the eleventh century, it is not until the beginning of the fourteenth century that its development can be followed in detail. At this time, like so many other houses on Mount Athos, it was pillaged and destroyed by the Catalan mercenaries. There is contemporary information concerning efforts made towards its reconstruction and the safeguarding of its properties. In an attempt to establish proprietary rights the Emperor John V Paleologos published a chrysobull (1351) where the name is written as Konstamonitou. The same form is found in the third *Typikon* of Mount Athos (1394) where the monastery ranked sixteenth amongst the twenty-five then extant, and again in a chrysobull of Manuel II Paleologos which, amongst other matters, defined its boundaries.

Amongst the benefactors and renovators of the monastery mention should be made of the Despot George Brankovič and the Princess of Serbia, Anne the Philanthropic. In addition to their many gifts and bequests of property, both presented Kastamonitou with several old monasteries such as Skamandrenou, Neakitou, St Hypatius and others. Radič, Commander-in-Chief of Serbia, who resigned his rank to become a monk here with the name Romanos, was also a liberal donor.

Despite all its patrons, the later years were not so prosperous at Kastamonitou. With the Turkish Occupation of Greek lands Kastamonitou experienced the same difficulties as the other monasteries. Heavy taxation in combination with other misfortunes precipitated a long and serious economic crisis. In 1666 Joseph, Metropolitan of Samos, gives us a bleak insight into the state of the monastery which, when he visited it, had six monks. During the abbacy of the hieromonach Gabriel a decree of the Patriarch Neophytos VII instituted the coenobitic way of life. But because of long continued poverty and instability the change was realised only in 1818 when Chrysanthos was appointed abbot and worked strenuously to restore the monastery.

In the same years, 1819-20, Vasiliki, wife of Ali Pasha, gave large sums of money to the abbot Chrysanthos, then in Jannina. He brought it to Kastamonitou and used it to restore a section of the monastery. Once again, however, the boundary disputes with neighbouring Docheiariou flared up to make difficulties for Kastamonitou. The monastery was only extricated from its difficulties when the monk Symeon, a man of high calibre, was appointed abbot. In the second half of the last century he amassed many donations, mainly from Russia, and worked consistently for the good of the monastery, a large section of which he succeeded in renovating. It was at this time that the north wing was built, the *katholikon* reconstructed and the monastery managed to pay off its heavy debts.

The present **katholikon**, dedicated to St Stephen, is post-Byzantine and was built between 1860 and 1871 on the site of the earlier church. It is the usual Athonite style, without frescoes. Its floors is laid with marble slabs and it has a marble iconostasis (1867).

In addition to the *katholikon* there are four chapels inside the monastery and another five outside. Those within the monastery are the chapels of Our Lady, of St Constantine, of All Saints and of St Nicholas. The chapel of Our Lady (1871) has an elegant and unusual carved wooden iconostasis on which hangs the miracle-working icon of the Virgin *Portaitissa* (of the gate). Her fame is derived from the miracles she worked during the abbot Symeon's alms-collecting journey to Russia in 1872-76. St Constantine's was used as the *katholikon* during the construction of the present church. It has some post-Byzantine frescoes, mostly in the naive style. The chapel of All Saints is a small attractive building and St Nicholas, comparatively large, is sited in the hospital infirmary.

The chapels which lie outside the monastery are: the Archangels, in the cemetery, which has an older sanctuary gate; the Holy Trinity, in a prominent position on raised ground; the Panagoudas, in the ravine, with some interesting post-Byzantine wall-paintings; St Antony, on the site of the former monastery of Neakitou, with a magnificent iconostasis dated to 1670 and, lastly, St Nicholas at the port. This chapel is no longer used, partly because it lies in territory claimed by both Kastamonitou and Docheiariou and partly because of a tale which says that a child was born there during the Greek War of Independence, when the defenceless population of Chalkidiki took shelter on the Mountain.

In Karyes Kastamonitou owns only one *kellion*, dedicated to the Athonite Fathers, where its representative of the Holy Assembly resides.

Kastamonitou has many treasures, of which the most valuable are the three miracle-working icons to be seen in the *katholikon*. One depicts the first

74. The entrance to the monastery on the south side.

martyr St Stephen, and probably dates to the eighth century. According to tradition, this icon arrived at Athos after a miraculous journey from Jerusalem at the time of the iconoclastic struggles. There are indications of burning on its lower edge, and above the left eye is a large crack. There are two icons of the Virgin, one of Our Lady *Hodegetria* (twelfth century) which some claim was a gift to the monastery from Anne the Philanthropic, the other of Virgin *Antiphonetria* (she who retorts). The legend attached to this icon is that on the eve of St Stephen's day, a jar which happened to be under the icon was filled with oil. It is still exhibited in the monastery. It is also said that the monk in charge of the storerooms was worried about the lack of oil on this feast day of the monastery, and that with this miracle the Virgin 'retorted', that is, she reassured him.

There is another small icon of St Stephen, dated to the sixteenth century, and a fragment of the True Cross. Kastamonitou possesses many holy relics contained in beautifully decorated and elegant reliquaries, crucifixes, sacerdotal vestments, ecclesiastical plate, a very fine *epitaphios*, a Gospel Book in silver-plated covers presented by Vasiliki, as well as many historically important chrysobulls, lead-sealed bulls and other documents.

The **library** is housed above the narthex of the *katholikon* and possesses 110 manuscripts, of which 14 are written on parchment. It contains also a large number of printed books.

The monastery of Kastamonitou occupies the twentieth place in the Athonite hierarchy and follows the coenobitic way of life and government. It now supports some thirty-five monks.

THE ART OF MOUNT ATHOS

Mount Athos, by reason of its wealth and variety in works of Byzantine art, is a living microcosm of that era. Each of the many manifestations of Byzantine art, be it architecture, painting, relief sculpture or miniature work in such materials as parchment, paper, metal, gold, ivory, wood or textiles, is represented here by an abundance of examples of splendid craftsmanship.

Until the Fall of Constantinople in 1453 the art of Mount Athos followed the artistic currents of Byzantium. Only in architecture, particularly with regard to the lay-out and external shaping of the *katholika*, did it develop a clearly Athonite style. Although painters began coming to Athos from the time of the Paleologue emperors, it was chiefly during the years of Turkish domination that they arrived in large numbers, leaving Constantinople in search of a refuge. Athos was left undisturbed by the conquerors and thus developed as a new artistic centre with its own iconographers, where, especially in painting, the Orthodox tradition was maintained, quite uninfluenced by Western trends.

Athos is not only a treasure house of architecture and monumental painting, but also of many precious portable icons of both the Byzantine and post-Byzantine periods. Furthermore, the monasteries amassed valuable manuscripts, precious relics and priceless gifts from the pious and devout Byzantine emperors, rulers of free or enslaved Orthodox countries, high ranking ecclesiastics and many humble Christians. These treasures, all of which bring to life the greatness of medieval Hellenism, have been reverently preserved, often in the midst of great dangers, by the continuous care of the Athonite fathers.

ARCHITECTURE

Seen from afar all the monasteries on Mount Athos and many of the coenobitic *sketae* give the impression of a small fortified medieval town. Their lay-out follows the typical plan of a Byzantine monastery, which is derived from older Eastern and Hellenistic prototypes. This style of construction was dictated by the need for the defence of the monks against many different external enemies.

The monastery buildings are surrounded by a wall which follows the contours of the ground, but which usually forms a four-sided enclosure. Only in a

75. Defence tower of a monastery (Karakalou).

143

76. An Athonite katholikon, exterior view (Great Lavra).

few instances is it polygonal. This wall is massively built, both thick and high, furnished at intervals with small turrets, crenellations, embrasures and machicolations. There is usually one strong and imposing tower at the highest, or the weakest, point of the enclosure. In its construction, as in all the other buildings which we shall examine later, there prevails the usual asymmetry and irregularity of Byzantine concept and execution.

The defence tower, or keep of the monastery, emphasises still further its fortified character. It served both as a watch-tower and as a last refuge for the fathers in the event of siege. These towers are normally very high, and are divided into several floors by wooden joists and planks. There is frequently a chapel on the top floor and a cistern at ground level. Rectangular in plan with a single entrance at first-floor level, these towers are marvels of medieval architecture and confer a distinctive external appearance on nearly all the Athonite monasteries.

The monastery has a single entrance, usually placed in the middle of one of the enclosure walls, with two gates at either end of the passageway formed by the thickness of the wall. These gates are closed by heavy wooden doors strengthened by iron strips and secured from inside by a heavy wooden bar, called the *zygos*. One monk, with the title of *pyloros* or *portaris*, is charged with special responsibility for the gates, and lives in a cell within

77. Interior of a refectory (Vatopedi).

the entrance. He shuts the gates every evening immediately after the setting of the sun and opens them again in the morning at sunrise. The passage is roofed by a barrel vault, or sometimes by a ribbed vault, above which rises a tower containing a chapel or a block of cells. At some monasteries a columned porch has been constructed in front of the entrance, but this is always a later addition.

A few monasteries also have a small second gate, the postern, which is often found in the wall opposite the main entrance. This postern was provided for reasons of defence and so that monks should have an escape route. It leads either to the gardens or the open mountainside.

Beyond the main entrance the courtyard of the monastery opens out. It is usually paved and its shape is dictated by the outline of the walls. According to the lie of the ground and to the exent of the monastery buildings, the court is either very large and spacious or it is cramped and restricted, sometimes being so narrow that it is little more than a series of passageways.

The *katholikon* or main church of the monastery is always found in the centre of the court, whereas the position of the *phiale*, the *refectory*, the smaller chapels, fountains, the various other necessary buildings and trees, usually cypresses, varies from monastery to monastery. Because there is no fixed and appointed place for these adjuncts they are placed wherever the lie of the ground permits. If space is really limited, they may be absent altogether or, if they are indispensable to the functioning of the community, be incorporated into one side of the quadrangle. There are some examples where restoration work has enlarged the area of the quadrangle, as at Chelandari, or has created a second, independent court, as at Gregoriou.

The **katholikon**, as the main church of the monastery is called, occupies the most honoured place in the architectural scheme, standing free on all sides, usually in the centre of the court, a position calculated to attract the reflections of the monks and inspire their activities. Except for the church of the Protaton and the *katholikon* of the monastery of Stavronikita, all the monastery churches are built in a similar style, following the plan of the oldest of them all, that of Great Lavra founded in 963. The plan is peculiar to the Holy Mountain, and has consequently been called the 'Athonite style'. It is based on the usual four-columned inscribed-cross church with dome, a form common in Constantinople. This model developed into the triple-apsed church, with the development of the two short arms of the cross into apses. These apses are called choirs because it is here that the cantors stand during the service. At its western end the *katholikon* terminates in a double narthex, that is to say an exo-narthex and a spacious eso-narthex or *lite,* so named from the prayers of mourning for the dead read here. On the north and south sides respectively are usually two small chapels, sometimes only one. These chapels are usually domed, the weight resting on four columns.

The definitive characteristics of this new style are thus the triple-apsed east end, the *lite* and the chapels added to one or both sides. One peculiarity of some of these churches should also be mentioned. It concerns the two rooms on either side of the sanctuary apse in which are situated the *prothesis* and the *diakonikon*. They are called the *typikaria*, and are usually circular inside and octagonal outside, as for example at Dionysiou.

This intricate arrangement was determined largely by liturgical requirements. Within its walls the Athonite church exhibits the transcendence of the Athonite monasteries as spiritual centres, and reflects the gradual and strenuous path its monks pursue towards their ultimate goal, the closer communion with God. All parts of the church are pervaded by the feeling of a striving for exaltation and of a progress to complete unity with the Spirit. It permeates the whole church from the narthexes to the innermost depths of the sanctuary, from side chapel to side chapel, from one choir to the other, as well as from iconostasis, to walls, arches and columns, even to the suspended radiant dome. This burgeoning of the soul in each dimension of the church, length, breadth and height, is much assisted by the murals which cover all the internal walls in most of the *katholika* on Athos. These paintings are placed according to strict Byzantine rules, and are divided into successive tiers, larger or smaller according to the size of the church. Christ Pantocrator is always represented in the dome as a symbol of his omniscient power over all.

Other features of the church on which special care has been lavished are the carved wooden iconostasis, the *proskynetaria* and stands for icons inlaid with mother-of-pearl, the wonderful marble *opus sectile* in the floors, and the marble revetment on the walls and the piers, the marble columns topped by ornate capitals, the bronze candelabra hanging by chains from the ceiling of the dome, and the sanctuary lamps.

The outside walls of most of the churches are distempered in red, and some are built in cloisonné masonry. Many of the façades are decorated with ceramic tiles, inlaid with patterns of rosettes, circles or spirals, while others con-

78. *Phiale for the blessing of the waters (Great Lavra).*

tain bas-reliefs or painted decoration and scenes. All the churches have lead-covered roofs, with the largest dome in the centre and many other subsidiary domes around it.

In addition to the *katholikon*, each monastery contains a number of smaller chapels. These are either free-standing buildings situated on one side of the court, or part of the other buildings making up the four sides of the monastery. In this case they are usually placed on the top floor.

The next most important building after the *katholikon* is the **refectory**, or dining room. Here the monks take their food communally. It is a free-standing building usually sited close to and opposite the church, slightly to the west. There are, however, monasteries where shortage of space has made it necessary for the refectory to be built into the south or west side of the monastery.

The refectories were intended to seat many monks and pilgrims, and are therefore very large. There is no consistency of plan, some being built in the shape of a cross, others resembling a T, others an elongated rectangle. They terminate in an apse in which the abbot's chair is placed on a raised dais. They are wooden-roofed, while the two or more rows of benches and tables may be of either wood or marble. All contain a small pulpit or reading desk from which, during mealtimes, the monk appointed as reader recites the several passages for the day.

The wall-paintings of the refectories are of great interest. Here one finds representations of the lives of saints, episodes from the life of Christ and the Virgin, the Twenty-four strophes of the Akathistos Hymn, the Heavenly Ladder, the Root of Jesse and many other scenes, while in the apse the most commonly found painting is the Last Supper.

Close to the refectory are found the service areas: the *hestia* or kitchen and the *magipeion* or bakery, and the ground floor or even basement *docheion* and cellars, that is to say the storerooms for dry food-stuffs and those for liquids such as wine and oil.

The *katholikon* and *refectory* together are considered the two most important buildings of the monastery, symbolising its communal aspect. Hence they usually form a unit.

Sometimes between these two buildings, occasionally at some other point in the court, but always close to the *katholikon*, is the **phiale** which serves for the ceremony of blessing the waters on the first of every month and the festival of the Baptism of Christ. The *phiale* is either circular or polygonal, ringed by eight columns closed in by a low parapet and supporting a hemispherical dome. In the centre is a marble fountain with several jets. The whole is usually constructed in white marble, with relief decorations on the parapet slabs. The inner surface of the dome is frequently painted with scenes connected with the Blessing of the Waters or the Baptism. It should be noted that at monasteries where space is limited a *phiale* is sometimes lacking.

The remaining many-storeyed buildings rise above the thick outer wall, with most of the windows looking into the court, thereby emphasising the fortress-like character of the monasteries. These buildings may belong to several periods, ranging from the fourteenth to the nineteenth century, but the majority were erected in the course of the eighteenth century. Many different architectural trends are represented within the general building scheme. The monastic buildings demonstrate many of the features of popular architecture in northern Greece. From the tiled roofs rise many small domes and a forest of chimneys which enhance the impression of size and lend enchantment and a picturesque quality to the distant view.

Of these buildings we would distinguish the administrative headquarters, which contain special rooms for offices, the council chamber, public reception rooms, the guest chambers or *archontarikion*, the hospital and the infirmary. On the lower levels and in the basements of the buildings are the storerooms, the oil press, grape press, the candle maker's and the tailor's workshops, and others, which are often less well-run than formerly.

The remainder of the buildings are made up of the cells which house the brothers, laid out sometimes in a single, sometimes in a double row of rooms. Usually these cells are placed on the outside wall, with a corridor running the length of the building looking into the court. Windows and balconies with a view away from the monastery are always indicative of later construction. In the coenobitic monasteries each monk lives in a single small room, sparsely furnished with a chair, a table and a bed. When the houses were still idiorrhythmic the monk may have occupied a suite of adjoining rooms which were often as well furnished as many flat in the secular world would be.

In addition to the defence tower of the monastery, of which we have already spoken, is the bell-tower. This is usually sited at some point in the courtyard as a free-standing unit; less frequently, it is built into the precinct wall.

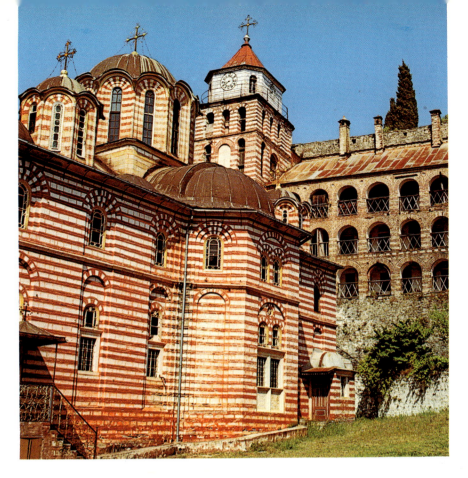

79. Range of cells looking inwards to the courtyard (Zographou).

They are usually square in plan, with a four-gabled wooden roof. On the top-most floors are single, sometimes double, openings, behind which hang a selection of bells in different sizes. One monk is in special charge of the bells (the *koudounokroustis* or *kabanaris)* and rings them with both hands and feet at the same time.

Immediately outside the monastery are various dependencies, small chapels, and monastic dwellings.

Close to the entrance, but outside, stands a small wooden booth or kiosk where the visitor may rest and refresh himself for a little before entering the monastery, a necessary step since he has frequently experienced a tiring hike from another monastery or from the port. It is also the point at which he will pick up his means of transport on his departure.

Somewhere close by lies the cemetery with its small chapel and ossuary. In the vicinity of the monastery lie its *kellia, kalyvae, kathismata* and hermitages.

A point of interest about the monasteries of Mount Athos, which should not be overlooked are the *arsanades* (ports). They are also called *tarsanades* and are small harbours used for mooring the boats which call from the outside world and for the caiques which serve the various needs of the monasteries. Every monastery has its port, sited in a small bay as close as possible to the monastery which it serves. At the port are usually a complex of storage buildings, a house for the monk in charge, space for the monastery's boats, a chapel, and a tower. The monks in charge of the harbours, and their traffic and commerce, live in these towers.

SCULPTURE

Unlike the painting, the sculpture on Mount Athos is very limited. This is true for all of Byzantium especially in the period after the iconoclastic controversy. It was during this time that monasticism appeared in its organised form on the Mountain, so that it is not surprising that we find very little sculpture in the Athonite monasteries.

Typical examples are to be found in an architectural context, for example as columns, column capitals, parapet slabs and relief plaques. All the classical orders can be found amongst the column capitals, while some of those which have been re-used are especially interesting. The same is true of the often multicoloured columns which we see in some later monuments on Athos.

The parapet slabs are usually found enclosing the basin of the *phiale,* which stands outside the church in the court. From an artistic and archaeological point of view, the most interesting are those of the *phiale* of Great Lavra, bearing bas-relief decoration with foliate and geometric patterns, rhomboids, circles, semi-circular patterns, crosses, rosettes and groups of birds. Similar plaques are to be found in the western façade of the *katholikon* of Lavra, below the glazing of the exo-narthex.

One of the finest examples of sculpture is the marble plaque bearing the figure of St Demetrios, built into the western wall of the *katholikon* of Xeropotamou. It probably dates to the Midde Byzantine period. The saint is depicted in a full-length frontal pose, wearing a mantle and holding a cross in his right hand. Tradition, as the later inscription bordering the panel tells us, claims that it was brought to Athos from Constantinople. Another opinion, however, maintains that it was brought from Thessalonica.

Marble or stone slabs with relief figures or simple decorative patterns are often in the façades and walls of the churches, and at many other points in the different buildings of the monasteries.

80. Re-used column capital in the katholikon of the monastery of Iveron.

81

81. The monastery of Xeropotamou. 18th-century relief representation of the monastery on one of the parapet slabs of the phiale.

82 - 83. Post-Byzantine reliefs in the exo-narthex of the katholikon of Great Lavra.

84. A Middle Byzantine relief set in the south-west corner of the narthex in the katholikon at the monastery of Xeropotamou, depicting St Demetrios.

85 - 86. Twelfth-century wall-paintings in the kellion of Ravdouchou, depicting the Apostles Peter and Paul.

PAINTING

It is well known that painting occupies the central place in Byzantine art and that it is in this form that Byzantine art realises its highest aesthetic achievements and its transcendental greatness. The Holy Mountain has been the greatest artistic centre of the Byzantine world at least since the years of the Paleologue dynasty and especially during the years of the Turkish Occupation, when it sustained the best of the Byzantine artistic traditions as it continues to do today.

When we speak of painting on Mount Athos, we mean not only the many examples of monumental art but also the multitude of excellent portable icons painted on wood and the priceless miniatures to be found in its illuminated manuscripts.

MONUMENTAL ART

In contrast with the architectural lay-out of the *katholika* which, as we saw, is standardised and may be characterised as 'Athonite', painting on Mount Athos follows the various artistic movements of successive ages. Many painters came to Athos from various places in both the Byzantine and the post-Byzantine periods, and worked on a considerable number of monuments many of which are still preserved today.

We should not lose sight of the fact that Athos produced its own hagiographical painters and consequently its own style, just as happened at other monastic centres in Constantinople and elsewhere. It is impossible to believe that all frescoes and portable icons were created by painters who converged on Athos from their several differing backgrounds and trainings. Even today on Mount Athos there are many hagiographical establishments and a significant number of monks painting on their own.

Almost the whole of the interior wall surfaces of most of the *katholika*, many of the smaller chapels and of the refectories are decorated with murals. The same is true of the *kyriakon* in the *sketae* and of many of the chapels in the monastic dependencies.

The themes depicted follow the well-known iconographical cycles of the Byzantine Church. The pictures are arranged in successive horizontal tiers, each incident in a particular cycle divided from the next by a border, so that each scene appears as a separate, self-contained picture. The artists did not simply paint single episodes or isolated faces, but tried to elevate man's soul from the earth and the visible world to the heavens and the spiritual realms, even to God himself, passing through different stages. This was achieved by the carefully planned juxtaposition of themes, as prescribed by the monk Dionysios of Fourna in his treatise *'The Painter's Manual'*.

When looking at any Athonite church, therefore, we should bear in mind the principles expounded by this writer, as well as the iconographical programme laid down for every Byzantine church. Everywhere we find the same arrangement of scenes, always in this order from the lower series to the upper. First of all are the representations of individual saints, holy men and ascetics; there follow scenes from the life and Passion of Christ and from the life of the Virgin, taken from the Gospels and the apocryphal Gospels. Higher up, on the pendentives of the dome, are the Four Evangelists; Matthew and John are always painted on the east because they speak respectively about the human and divine nature of Christ. Beyond them, on the apse of the sanctuary, stands the Virgin *Platytera*, the Divine Liturgy, the Communion of the Apostles and the great Fathers of the Church. Finally on the tympanum of the dome is the representation of the Deesis, angels and prophets, and at the highest point of the church, the concave inner suface of the dome which symbolises the heavens, Christ Pantocrator.

Most of the buildings on Athos have been restored at different periods, with the result that their frescoes have been retouched one or more times, according to the repairs carried out.

The oldest paintings to have survived date from the twelfth century. They are the pictures of the apostles Peter and Paul together with some other scenes at the *kellion* of Ravdouchou near Karyes, below the monastery of Koutloumousiou. Some thirteenth-century fragments are preserved in a small apse of an earlier chapel below a newer building at the *kellion* of the Holy Trinity belonging to Chelandari.

Two separate trends in painting can be distinguished. They belong to two different eras and derive from traditions foreign to the Holy Mountain. The one is related to the so-called *Macedonian School,* which flourished in the dual centres of Constantinople and Thessalonica. It developed and was practised largely in the northern provinces of the Byzantine Empire in the late thirteenth and the first half of the fourteenth century. The other, more conservative, is that of the *Cretan School.* Its roots are also in models of Constantinople, but both on Mount Athos and elsewhere it reached the peak of its creativity in the sixteenth century, although its origins are far earlier.

Examples of the art of the Macedonian School are to be found in the church of the Protaton, whose frescoes are attributed to its chief representative, Manuel Panselinos, and in the *katholikon* of the monastery of Chelandari, which was painted by the famous artists Michael Astrapas and Eutychios. Both examples are dated to the early fourteenth century. The general characteristics of these murals, which differ a little in technique, are realism, naturalistic and mobile expression in the faces, the dramatised appearance and bright colours. All these elements together tend to build up a metaphysical atmosphere. The murals in the *katholikon* of Vatopedi belong to the same century, as do those in two small chapels at the monastery of Chelandari, St George and the Annunciation of the Virgin in the cemetery.

Works of the Cretan School date mostly to the sixteenth century, and are to be found in many of the *katholika,* small chapels and refectories on Mount Athos. Many of its painters came to Athos seeking refuge and a suitable place in which to practise their traditional art after the Fall of the Constantinople and the Turkish Occupation of the Empire.

The finest examples of the art of this School are the frescoes of the *katholikon* of Great Lavra (1535) and of Stavronikita (1546). Both churches were decorated by the most famous representative of the School, Theophanes the Cretan; their frescoes are considered to be his most mature works. At Stavronikita he was assisted by his son Symeon. Other examples are the *katholika* of Dionysiou (1547) and Docheiariou (1568) decorated by the Cretan Tzorzis; of Xenophontos (1544), decorated by another Cretan, Antonios, and the chapel of St Nicholas at Great Lavra (1560), decorated by Frangos Katellanos. Although Katellanos is said to have been a pupil of the Cretan masters, his work bears little resemblance to theirs, exhibiting an independence of its own. Many other Athonite murals are attributed to Cretan painters; for example, in the *katholikon* of Koutloumousiou (1540), the chapel of St George at the monastery of St Paul (1555), and the refectories at Great Lavra (first half of the sixteenth century) and Philotheou (1540).

87. *St Theodore Stratelates. Wall-painting in the church of the Protaton. Early 14th century.*

88. *Praising the Lord; a wall-painting in the chapel of the Virgin Koukouzelissa at the monastery of Great Lavra. 18th century.* →.

89

89. *Detail from the Mocking of Christ; a wall-painting of the 18th century.*

90. *Detail from a 16th-17th-century wall-painting in the katholikon at the monastery of Dionysiou.*

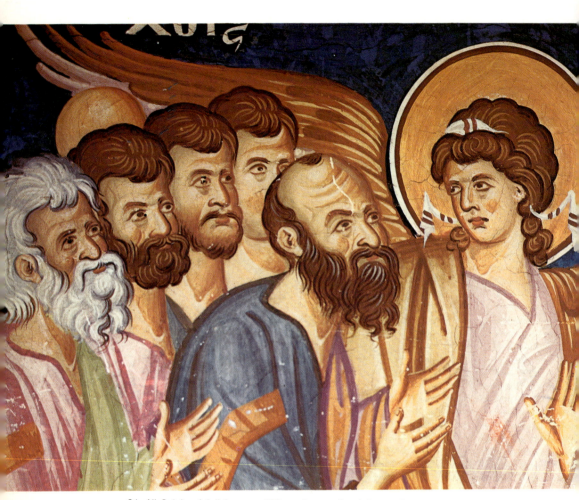

91. All Saints; detail from an 18th-century wall-painting in the chapel of St Demetrios in the monastery of Vatopedi.

The chief characteristics of the Cretan School compared with those of the Macedonian School are the more restrained gestures and movements, the simplicity, and the calm and noble stances of the figures. Their austere appearance is depicted in shadowy colours against a dark background with a few lines to pick out the protruding surfaces. An almost invisible line, rather than shading, defines the outlines of the figures. It is a stern and conservative art which, although it maintains the idealism of the Byzantine tradition, blends old and new elements into new forms. This Cretan style was long followed on Athos, even as late as the beginning of the last century, although it had lost the originality and creativity of its earlier masters.

After the acme of the Cretan School had passed, it is possible to say that the two traditions, Cretan and Macedonian, fused, at least on Mount Athos. In the first decades of the eighteenth century, the painter Dionysios of Fourna,

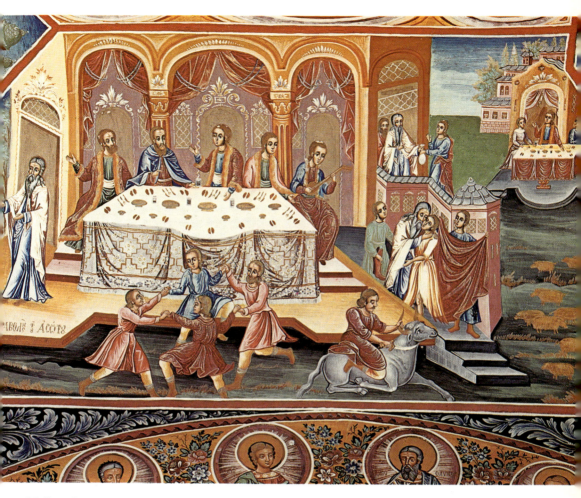

92. Narrative painting of the Parable of the Prodigal Son; 19th-century wall-painting in the monastery of Great Lavra.

whom we mentioned above, taught a return to the techniques of Panselinos. But Western mannerisms, especially after their introduction and adoption in the Ionian Islands and other regions of Greece, were also brought to Athos. Particularly in the last two centuries of the Turkish Occupation they infuenced the style of its painting. Only in recent years have Athonite painters, whether working in isolation or as members of a team belonging to one of the hagiographical houses, begun to return to the original Byzantine models.

Within this section on monumental art we must not omit mention of the mosaics built into the walls of the *katholikon* of Vatopedi. Dated to the years of the Comnenian dynasty, they are of very great interest and unique of their kind on Athos. They include a representation of the Annunciation, with the Virgin and the angel Gabriel across from one another above the eastern columns of the nave, the Deesis above the entrance to the eso-narthex and, below this, a second depiction of the Annunciation.

PORTABLE ICONS

The monasteries of Mount Athos possess a very large number of portable icons ranging in date from the Byzantine period to the present day. They are painted on wooden panels, and are stored either in special rooms, or in the treasuries of the monasteries, or in the *katholika* and small chapels. The most popular image is that of Our Lady, the *Theotokos,* who is especially revered by the Athonite monks, and these icons are considered amongs the richest treasures of Mount Athos.

Many of the icons are dated to the later centuries of the Byzantine Empire, the period of the Paleologue dynasty. However, most of those of which we shall make special mention were painted by Cretan artists in the post-Byzantine period, and the stylistic characteristics of the Cretan School are clearly distinguishable. The tradition of icon painting is even more conservative and austere than the wall-paintings by the same School. Such icons are stripped of the detail employed by the Paleologue artists and portray only the figures essential to the composition. During the Turkish Occupation, irrespective of whether their subject was an icon for special veneration or narrative icons, artists tried more than ever before to continue the Orthodox faith and tradition and to depict the beliefs of the Church to whose service they were dedicated.

Many tales circulate on Mount Athos to explain the creation, the arrival, the distinguishing titles and, most of all, the miracle-working qualities of many of its icons. According to these tales some of the icons were 'not made by human hands'; others are attributed to St Luke. These icons, in which the monasteries take special pride, are usually displayed on *proskynetaria* in the *katholika* or in chapels named after the icons. The monks relate many tales and legends concerning the arrival of these icons on Mount Athos, saying that they came in a miraculous fashion as gifts from various places, but mainly Constantinople. The most common version is that they travelled to Athos over the sea, having been committed to the waves by their former owners in an attempt to save them from the destructive fury of the iconoclasts, and later, from infidel conquerors. A number of legends surround the naming and miracle-working qualities of many icons, especially those of the Virgin; some of these are referred to above in the descriptions of the individual monasteries.

A multitude of portable icons is to be found on the high *templa* or iconostases of the churches. These iconostases are made up of successive tiers of niches in which icons are placed, following a traditional order still observed. The largest icons are placed in the most commanding positions. Thus the despotic icons, Christ and the Virgin Mary, are followed by St John the Baptist and the saint to whom the church is dedicated. The Royal Doors carry the representation of the Annunciation of the Virgin. Higher up is a second row of smaller icons selected from the calendar of feast days in the ecclesiastical year, the despotic icons, those concerning the Mother of God and the saints' festivals. There follow the apostolic icons (those showing the apostles), and a representation of the Deesis in the centre. Above, at the highest point, is a large crucifix on which is painted the Crucifixion, and, on the arms of the cross, the symbols of the four Evangelists.

Worthy of note are the important collections of icons owned by the monas-

93. Christ Pantocrator; 13th-century icon from the large collection kept in the treasury of the monastery of Chelandari.

94

94 - 95. Sts George and Demetrios; mosaic icon in the new katholik(
the monastery of Xenophontos. 13th century.

96. Virgin Hodegetria; mosaic icon of the 12th-13th century in the m
stery of Chelandari.

97. St John the Theologian; mosaic icon in the treasury of the mona
of Great Lavra. 13th century.

96

95

98 - 99. *Two of the miracle-working icons of Our Lady on Mount Athos; Virgin Koukouzelissa (Great Lavra) and the Virgin Portaitissa (Iveron).*

teries of Great Lavra, Vatopedi, Iveron, Chelandari, Pantokrator, Koutloumou-siou, St Paul's and Karakalou. Yet others are those on the post-Byzantine icon-ostasis in the church of the Protaton (1542), the famous cycle of the Twelve Feasts at Stavronikita (1546), the Great Deesis, consisting of five icons by the painter Euphrosynos at Dionysiou (1542), a series of apostolic icons in the new *katholikon* at Xenophontos, and many others.

    Also the mosaic icons: Christ the Saviour at Esphigmenou, the Virgin *Hode-getria* at Chelandari, the Crucifixion, St Anne and the Virgin and others at Vatopedi, St John the Evangelist at Great Lavra, St Nicholas *Streidas* at Stav-ronikita and Saints George and Demetrios at Xenophontos.

100. Presentation of the Virgin in the Temple; icon of the
14th century.

101. Portable icon of the 16th
century with a representation
of the Transfiguration of the
Saviour from the monastery
of Pantokrator.

ILLUMINATED MANUSCRIPTS

Art on Mount Athos is not confined simply to the ornamentation and embellishment of its churches. The monastery libraries contain more than 15,000 manuscripts, written on parchment, bombasine and paper, which form one of the richest collections in the world. Of these works of art in themselves, more than 1800 are illuminated. Those on parchment, especially, often contain rich decoration.

These illuminated manuscripts date from the ninth and tenth centuries and for the most part contain religious and ecclesiastical subject matter. In particular they comprise the texts of the Old and New Testaments, the Psalter, the Octateuch (i.e. the first eight books of the Old Testament), the text of the Four Gospels (a Gospel Book), extracts from the Gospels read during church services throughout the ecclesiastical year (Gospel Lectionary), Menologia (a register of saints and their lives), various Homilies and, finally, theological writings. Only a small number of secular manuscripts have survived in comparison with the others, some 600 in all, and few are illuminated.

The illustration of the manuscripts which we shall now examine consists of miniature scenes, headpieces, initial letters and other decoration. The scenes may include a portrait of the author of the text and narrative pictures relating to the contents or occasionally to some other source. The illuminations, whether they occupy the whole or only part of the page, or are confined to the margin, are found at different points throughout the manuscript.

The headpieces at the beginning of the text are either rectangular, square, (in the form of a gate or of a Greek capital Π), round or band-shaped. Their decoration, like that of the capital letters, especially in the manuscripts of the Middle Byzantine period, is particularly rich, with polychrome foliate decoration and geometrical patterns. It is also common to find small animals, fish and birds grouped together, and occasionally even human figures or tiny scenes from daily life.

The miniatures usually combine aesthetic sensitivity with the expression of Christian faith and piety. All are works executed with great skill, and we may say that they have frequently served as the inspiration for the murals of Athonite and other churches.

The finest collections of illuminated manuscripts belong to the oldest and biggest monasteries on Mount Athos, namely Great Lavra, Vatopedi, and Iveron. Dionysiou, Koutloumousiou, Pantokrator, Stavronikita, Esphigmenou and St Panteleimon also contain some fine manuscripts, and the remaining houses are not without at least some texts. Many of the manuscripts now found in Athonite libraries were brought from Constantinople, and are examples of a highly developed and delicate art.

Some of the more important are mentioned in the section on the library of the monastery which owns them.

102. St John the Evangelist with Prochorus; representation in a Lectionary belonging to the monastery of Dionysiou. 11th century.

103

104

A few monasteries possess liturgical scrolls written on parchment, some of which are illuminated, for example Lavra (no. 2), Dionysiou (nos. 101 and 105), with scenes, headpieces, and elaborate initial letters.

Miniature painting occurs also in another form, on the interesting diptychs owned by the monasteries of Chelandari and St Paul. Similarly it is to be seen on the great wooden crucifix of St Paul's and on two frames at the monastery of Zographou.

103. Miniature in the margin of a Menologion in the monastery of Esphigmenou. It depicts the third day of the struggle of the eleven tribes of Israel with the tribe of Benjamin before Gibeah. 11th century.

104. Pastoral scene; a miniature in the margin of a Menologion belonging to the monastery of Esphigmenou. 11th century.

105. Scene of the Nativity in a Lectionary, the so-called 'Gospel of Nicephoros Phocas' kept in the treasury of Great Lavra. 11th century.

105

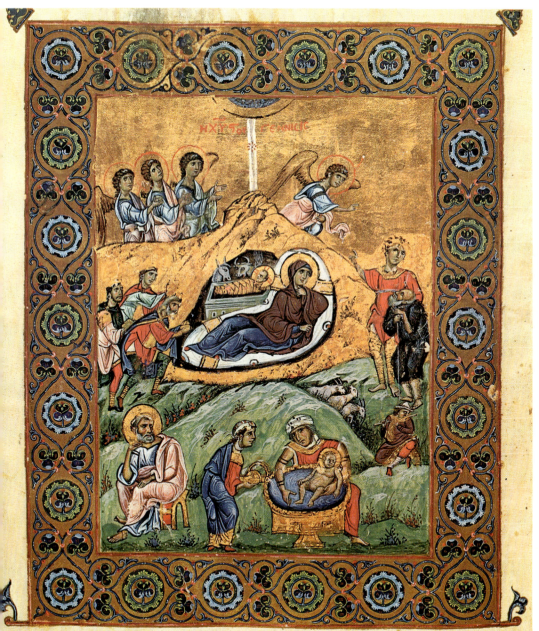

106. Headpiece and initial letter E which takes the shape of the figure of the Evangelist Luke. From a Gospel Book belonging to the monastery of Dionysiou. 11th century.

107. *The prayer of Jesus in Gethsemane. Below, initial letter E: Jesus teaching his disciples.*
From a Lectionary belonging to the monastery of Dionysiou. 11th century.

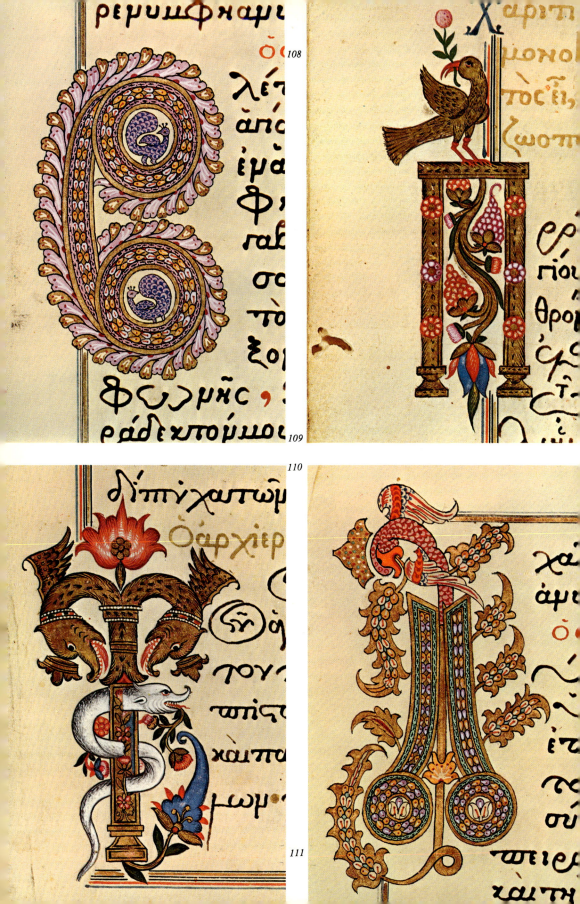

ρεμυμφηαμ

ὁ

λέγ
ἀπ
ἐμα
Φ
ταυ
σα
τὸ
ξο

Φωνῆς,
ράδεχπούμ

Χ
μονοι
τος εἴ,
ζωοπ

ερ,
ριοι
θρορ
ὑ
τ

δίπυχατῶμ
Ὁ ἀρχιερ

ὁ
του
πιστ
καπ
ωρ

χα
ἀμ
ὁ

ετ
οὐ
πιερ
ειμ
χαιτη

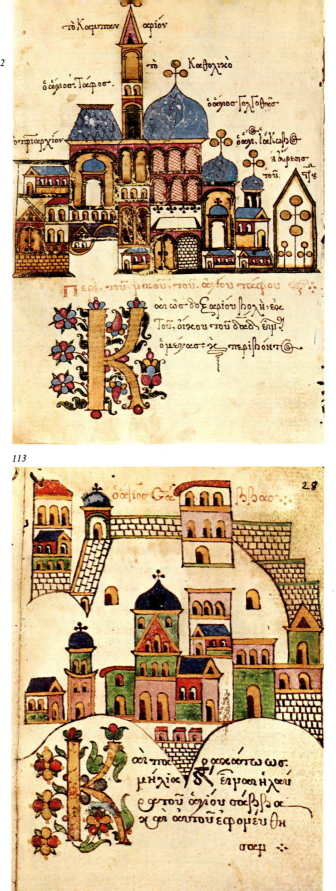

113

108. Initial letter B, embellished with foliage. Within the two circles are two peacocks. From a codex, the Akathistos Hymn, belonging to the monastery of Iveron. 17th century.

109. Initial letter Π, embellished with bunches of grapes, flowers and a bird perching on the cross-bar. From a codex in the monastery of Iveron. 17th century.

110. Initial letter T; above the schematised upper part of the letter are the heads of two winged dragons and a flower pattern. A serpent winds round the branch. From a codex in the monastery of Iveron. 17th century.

111. Initial letter Π, decorated with leafy branches and flowers. On the upper part of the letter is a winged dragon. From a codex, the Akathistos Hymn, belonging to the monastery of Iveron. 17th century.

112. Representation of the Holy Sepulchre and other buildings in Jerusalem, an initial letter K. From a proskynetarion to the Holy Land in the library of the monastery of Gregoriou. 17th century.

113. The famous Lavra of St Savvas in Palestine, an initial letter K. From a proskynetarion to the Holy Land in the library of the monastery of Docheiariou. 17th century.

MINIATURE ART

Many rare and interesting small works of art are preserved in the rich treasuries of the monasteries of Mount Athos. Thus there are carvings in various media – stone, wood, ivory – the products of goldsmiths, silversmiths, jewellers, enamellers and bronzesmiths, and the work of seamstresses and embroideresses. Many of these articles are still unknown and unpublished. Of the known works the finest are: the paten 'of Pulcheria' in the monastery of Xeropotamou, the small icon of the Virgin and of Saints George and Demetrios at Great Lavra, of the Crucifixion (inserted in the cover of a manuscript, no. 27) at Dionysiou, of the Transfiguration at Xenophontos, of St George at Vatopedi, and many others. All of these are carved on steatite or serpentine and are considered masterpieces of Byzantine art in this field.

The paten, reputedly presented by Pulcheria, belongs to the type known as *panagiaria* and depicts the Divine Liturgy. In the centre is the Virgin of the type known as *Vlachernitissa*. The archangels Michael and Gabriel, dressed in deacon's robes, stand on either side, swinging censers. This central group is enclosed by two concentric circles; in the inner are angels, priest and deacons while in the outer are saints and angels prostrate before the heavenly throne (the *Hetoimasia* or the preparation of the Throne for the Second Coming). All these tiny figures are encompassed within a diameter of 0.15 m. Executed with great skill and artistry, it is one of the finest Byzantine miniature works. The same delicacy is shown in the other works we listed above.

A special skill belonging to Mount Athos and still practised by its monks today, is the art of wood-carving. Their products are the very fine *templa* of the *katholika* and many small chapels – often with scenes from the Old and New Testaments and florid foliate decoration – reading desks, the *proskynetaria*, chests and crucifixes. The finely carved front cover of one of the manuscripts (no. 33) at Dionysiou is highly valued for its delicate execution and its wealth of scenes.

There are two sets of doors cast in bronze which bear designs and scenes in relief, those of the *katholika* of Great Lavra and Vatopedi. Other bronze articles include ecclesiastical plate, hanging lamps and candelabra, and other similar objects.

The only example of ivory work we shall mention is the magnificent small icon depicting the Crucifixion owned by Dionysiou.

The monasteries of Mount Athos boast many exquisite examples of craftsmanship of the Byzantine goldsmith, the enameller and the engraver of many different kinds of precious stones. Such items are sacred plate, rich covers for Gospels, haloes which decorate the miracle-working and other icons, and the gold and silver caskets studded with gems and decorated with small icons, which hold crucifixes containing fragments of the True Cross *(stavrothekes)* or the relics of saints *(leipsanothekes)*.

Of the cases containing crucifixes, which usually take the form of a many-domed church, special mention is to be made of that of Great Lavra, said to be the gift of the Emperor Nicephoros Phocas. Other outstanding examples are to be seen at Vatopedi, Chelandari, Koutloumousiou, Xeropotamou and St Paul's. Of the reliquaries we note that containing the bones of St Nephon at Dionysiou, and other fine ones at Vatopedi, Iveron, St Paul's and Simonopetra.

114. The Crucifixion carved in ivory. Monastery of Dionysiou. 10th century.

115. The wood-carved cover of a Psalter belonging to the monastery of Dionysiou. 13th century.

116. Small steatite icon with a representation of the Transfiguration of Christ, belonging to the monastery of Xenophontos. 12th century.

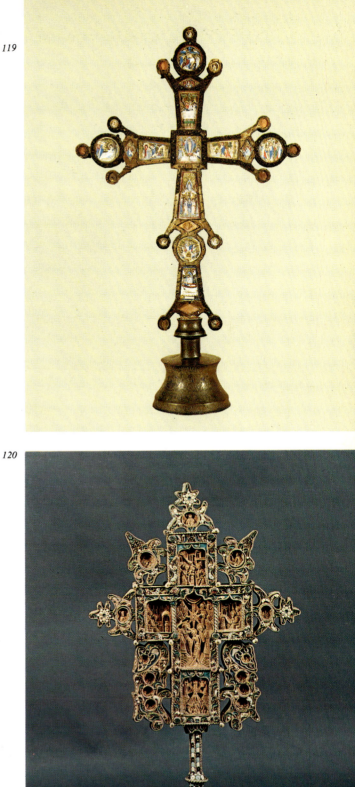

117. A steatite paten of the panagiaria type, the so-called 'paten of Pulcheria'. Monastery of Xeropotamou.

118. The reliquary containing the bones of St Nephon, Patriarch of Constantinople, made in the shape of a church. It belongs to the monastery of Dionysiou. 16th century.

119. Wooden cross decorated with miniatures in the monastery of St Paul. 13th century.

120. Cross owned by the monastery of Iveron. 18th century.

VESTMENTS AND GOLD-EMBROIDERED FABRICS

Nearly all the Athonite monasteries, and many of their dependencies, own richly embroidered ecclesiastical vestments and fabrics. They are most commonly woven of silk, embroidered with gold, silver or wire thread and are used either to decorate the sanctuary and to perform a liturgical function along with other sacerdotal objects, or they are part of the rich vestments used by the priests. Thus it is possible to divide the textiles into two categories. The first are the liturgical cloths which are used to perform an integral part of the services, such as the *epitaphios* (a holy shroud decorated with a representation of the Body of Christ), the *aeras* (chalice and paten veil), the curtain in front of the central entrance to the sanctuary and the cloths which cover the *proskynetaria*. The second category includes the priestly vestments and those worn by the three grades of monk when they participate in the various ceremonies, especially the divine liturgy. Amongst these garments are the hieratical *sakkos* (a garment slit at the sides and hanging to the knees), the great and the little *omophorion* (a long broad band of silk embroidered with crosses and an image of Christ), the *epitrachilion* (the priest's stole), the *orarion* (the deacon's stole or pectoral), the *epimanikia* (detachable cuffs, maniples) and the *epigonation* (a rhomboidal piece of cloth worn by ecclesiastical dignitaries at knee-level).

Such embroideries have preserved the Byzantine traditions undistorted and display exceptionally high standards of workmanship together with a choice of themes appropriate to the use of each article. They often bear the name of the donor, mostly high-ranking clergy, or of the embroideress.

The monasteries of Mount Athos have large numbers of these masterpieces of the Byzantine and post-Byzantine period, protecting them from many dangers, particularly from fires and pirate raids. It is especially amazing that any of these objects should have come down to us when we recall that we are talking about delicate materials, easily destroyed. As the most outstanding examples of embroidery we may cite two episcopal *sakkoi*, one belonging to Great Lavra and the other to Iveron, considered respectively to have belonged to the Emperors Nicephoros Phocas and John Tzimisces, and the *epitaphioi*, at the monasteries Kastamonitou, Stavronikita, Gregoriou, Pantokrator, Dionysiou and Zographou.

121 - 122. Embroidered maniples; one shows the Archangel Gabriel, the other the Communion of the Apostles.

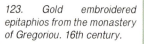

123. *Gold embroidered epitaphios from the monastery of Gregoriou. 16th century.*

ΘΡΗΝΟC

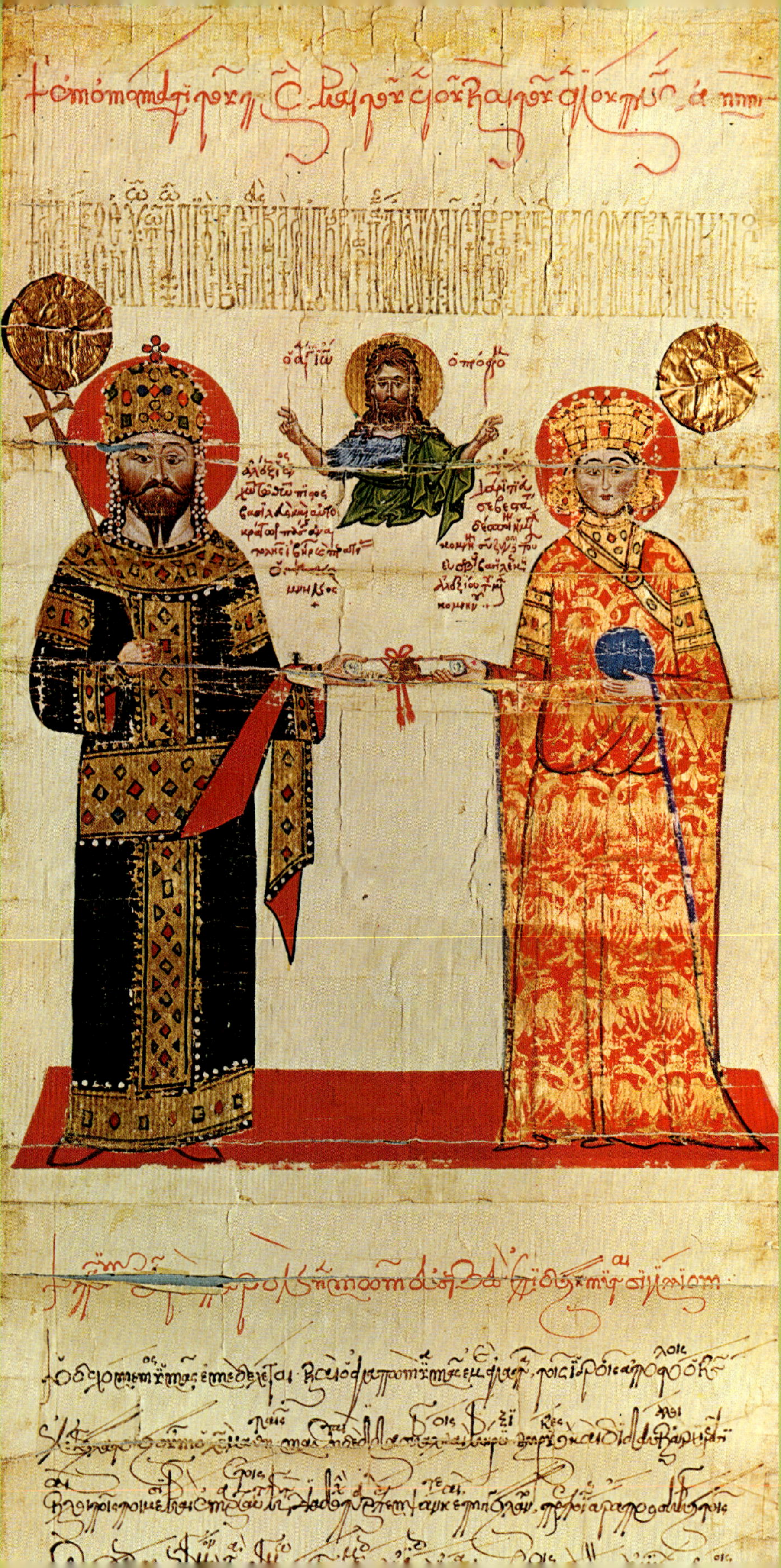

OTHER TREASURES

To complete the catalogue of treasures found on Mount Athos some of the many objects of veneration possessed by each monastery must be mentioned. The most important of these are the Fragments of the True Cross and the relics of many saints. Many monasteries own items connected with the life of Christ. Thus St Paul's owns the Gifts of the Magi, gold, frankincense and myrrh, Philotheou one of the nails of the Cross, Chelandari part of the Crown of Thorns and the shroud of Christ, while Vatopedi has other objects connected with the Passion of Christ, as well as the girdle of Our Lady.

All these treasures have been guarded by the Athonite fathers with infinite care and piety. They are shown only occasionally to visitors who have a special reason for venerating them.

As historic treasures of the Holy Mountain, we would mention a part of the tent of the Emperor Napoleon, belonging to Esphigmenou, and the many gifts of Byzantine emperors, other rulers and humble believers. Amongst these are a cup given by the Emperor Manuel II Paleologos to Vatopedi, made of jasper with a golden base, its two handles fashioned in the shape of snakes and studded all over with precious stones; the iron staff belonging to St Athanasios the Athonite and his iron cross which, following an ancient tradition, is worn by every newly tonsured monk at Great Lavra; and a multitude of episcopal staffs, many made of amber, pectorals mitres, patens, ecclesiastical plate, crucifixes studded with diamonds and other precious stones, and the many other objects to by found in almost every monastery.

The archives preserve many valuable documents connected either with the founding of the house or with the history of its renovations. These documents include *Typika*, chrysobulls, lead-sealed bulls, patriarchal decrees, documents concerning the foundation, acquisitions of property and dedications, and, lastly, Turkish firmans. Apart from their value as treasures, these documents provide invaluable information about the historical beginnings and development of monastic life on Mount Athos.

It may be supposed that even this profusion of rare and precious things does not exhaust the resources of the monastic treasuries of Mount Athos. Much may yet remain undiscovered to delight future scholars. Only a thorough search and complete study of the Athonite archives and other treasures, known and unknown, will fully and finally reveal the history and the art of Mount Athos and the quality of Athonite monasticism over the millennium of its existence.

124. Chrysobull issued by the Emperor Alexios III Comnenos, in the monastery of Dionysiou.

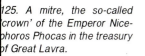

125. A mitre, the so-called crown' of the Emperor Nice-phoros Phocas in the treasury of Great Lavra.

126. One of the many episcopal mitres preserved in the treasuries of the mona-stery of Xeropotamou.

127. An episcopal staff made of amber, one of the treasures of the monastery of Xeropo-tamou.

128. The seven-branched lamp-stand in the shape of a lemon tree, in the katholikon of Iveron.

129. *Precious cover for a Lectionary, the 'Gospel of Nicephoros Phocas', to be found in the rich treasury of Great Lavra.*

130. The massive covering for a Russian Gospel in the library of the monastery of Iveron.

131. *Scenes showing the enthroned Christ between the Virgin and St John the Evangelist.*
Painting on glass in the monastery of St Paul.

132. The leaf of a diptych, showing twelve miniatures of the 13th century. Monastery of Chelandari.

EPILOGUE

This brief presentation of the history, the art and the life of Athonite monasticism attempts to give an insight into the unique nature of the Holy Mountain and the important role it has played in the life of the Greek Nation and the Greek Orthodox Church.

Mount Athos represents for the Greeks the cradle of national tradition and that part of Greece where, for more than a thousand years, the Greek-Christian heritage, Greek letters, and the true Byzantine style of worship have been preserved. Moreover, it is a sacred repository which contains untapped sources for the study of theology, philosophy, history, Byzantine and post-Byzantine art and Eastern mysticism. It is also a museum richly stocked with artistic treasures of the Christian Orthodox past.

Just as the granite rocks of Athos have withstood the incessant fury of the waves, so Athonite monasticism, the only state of God on earth, has clung obstinately to the dictates of the Church Fathers. Staunch bulwark of Orthodoxy, it has kept the Church untainted by heresy, uninfiltrated by any Western influence and true to the old traditions of worship. The names of the Byzantine emperors resound in the churches, and the sense of the past is so intense that the visitor to Mount Athos fast loses touch with the present and feels drawn into the continuity of the Byzantine traditions.

Patience and hope, together with prayer and the other monastic virtues, have always been the mainstays of the Athonite monks who lived and continue to live in these centuries-old monasteries of the Mountain. No power of this world has ever succeeded in deflecting them from their goal of eternal bliss, despite the difficulties and the many dangers which they have faced, because 'their strength is in adversity'.

Athos has remained *abatos* through the centuries, a divine gift of the Virgin, under whose protection the place has turned into a sanctuary imbued with holiness and a greatness not of this world. Her divine presence has pervaded everything, permeating the deep silence of the Mountain, while the monks, humble and devoted servants of God, are the only ones to receive her blessing and permission to live in her garden. A garden, where, like an unfading flower, the hallowed practices are cherished, the cultural contribution of Eastern Christianity is piously protected and the traditions of the Byzantine Empire are still the daily ritual. It is indeed a holy place, where the way of life is that dictated by the transcendental truths of mysticism, of prayer and of the life hereafter.

The unrivalled natural beauties of the Athos peninsula are those which make the greatest impression. The idyllic slopes are forested with firs, chestnuts, oaks and other trees, as well as dense green bushes. The heights of Athos itself dominate the whole; austere and eternal, it casts its shadow over the entire monastic state, a phenomenon unique in the world, a true physical and spiritual paradise.